t8

# OVER THE EDGE

## The First Ten Years

*An anthology of fiction and poetry*

*Edited by Susan Millar DuMars*

Salmon

Published in 2013 by
Salmon Poetry
Cliffs of Moher, County Clare, Ireland
Website: www.salmonpoetry.com
Email: info@salmonpoetry.com

ISBN 978-1-908836-53-3

THE OVER THE EDGE LOGO WHICH APPEARS ON THE COVER
AND ON THE TITLE PAGE WAS DESIGNED BY PAUL CONWAY

COVER ARTWORK: © Pat138241 | Dreamstime.com
COVER DESIGN, TYPESETTING & LAYOUT: Siobhán Hutson
PRINTED IN IRELAND BY Sprint Print, Dublin

Salmon Poetry gratefully acknowledges the support of The Arts Council

Fondly dedicated to the memory of

*Kevin Donnelly*
*Tom Duddy*
*Gerry Galvin*
*Paddy Henry*
*Michael Maye*
and
*Dennis O'Driscoll*

Over the Edge wishes to thank Dawn Wisniewski for her friendship and invaluable help with this project. We're grateful to Paul Conway for creating the OTE logo. We also want to thank retired County Librarian Pat McMahon for his years of support of Over the Edge.

We are very grateful to Sheila Duddy, and Marie and Cristina Galvin, for their kind assistance in choosing poems by Tom Duddy and Gerry Galvin.

# PREFACE
by Eamonn Wall

Poet and Smurfit-Stone Professor of Irish Studies
at the University of Missouri, St. Louis

*Over the Edge: The First Ten Years* is a timely celebration of both the Over the Edge reading series and the work of poets and fiction writers whose work was first showcased at the Thursday night readings hosted by Susan Millar DuMars and Kevin Higgins at the Galway City Library. Encouraged by Over the Edge, many of the writers present in this anthology have gone on to publish their first books with major presses and, subsequently, be nominated for prestigious national and international literary awards.

This anthology provides a generous selection of work and a lively introduction from Millar DuMars that locates the series within the contexts and histories of the Galway literary scene from the 1990's to the present.

Ably curated by Millar DuMars and Higgins, Over the Edge has remained faithful to its founding objective of "providing a showcase for writers who have not yet published a book," and remained an inclusive, social, educational, and welcoming occasion. Over the Edge has continued to thrive and develop: today, in addition to the Thursday night readings, Over the Edge hosts a Fiction Slam, an annual Poetry Showcase, an open mic event at the Westside Arts Festival, provides sponsorship for the literary magazine Skylight47, and works with adults with intellectual disabilities through its Away with Words–Over the Edge initiative.

The reach of Over the Edge has grown long and most impressive with the result that its renown has spread large and wide. In common with other important cultural institutions in Galway

(Macnas and Druid spring to mind), Over the Edge's strength is derived from its independent spirit and its inclusive heart.

It's exciting always to walk into Galway City Library for an Over the Edge reading – to hear emerging writers reading alongside published peers. I have never left less than wholly energized and full of a sense that writing has come alive again; furthermore, it's a real treat to read in *Over the Edge: The First Ten Years* many of the poems I heard for the first time read aloud in the City Library. What this anthology makes quite clear is the notable quality of work that has been written and read over the past decade. We are reminded that Over the Edge is a metier of both opportunity and quality.

# Contents

# INTRODUCTION

## *Standing on the Couch*
### by Susan Millar DuMars

In 2003 my partner Kevin and I were living in a grotty upstairs flat in Salthill, Galway. Wood panelling prevailed. A coin-op electricity metre ticked off our minutes of space-heating, television, light. We could watch the undulations of Galway Bay from our front window – if we stood on the couch and squinted.

We were both writers, though neither of us had yet published a book. Kevin's work had been showcased in chapbooks and pamphlets alongside other budding Galway writers. He and the poet Mike Begnal had founded the Burning Bush literary magazine; I met Kevin after submitting poems to the first issue. I'd been teaching creative writing, primarily in an evening course at a local community college, for a few years. Prior to that, I'd completed a long-term poetry writing project with young adults who had learning difficulties.

There'd been a flurry of literary activity in Galway in the late nineties. A café called Apostasy had hosted an anarchic weekly open mic for writers (the late Niall Rivers shambling in to declare, "I wrote this poem on the way here."). A basement wine bar called O'Ché's held similar events. A low-budget and intermittently produced literary magazine called *The Mag* had been born of the Apostasy movement. *The Burning Bush* appeared in 1999. That same year, Fred Johnston organised a daytime series called "Lunch on the Island" at which most of us read. The nationally recognised poets Rita Ann Higgins and Eva Bourke were still occasional attendees at the Galway Writers' Workshop, which met Saturdays in the Bridge Mills (from the Workshop was born *Crannóg* literary magazine, started, like Over the Edge, in 2003 and better and stronger than ever now, ten years later). Eva and Rita Ann had of course gotten their start through Salmon Poetry, also begun in Galway back in 1981. In 2002, the National University of Ireland's Galway campus launched its MA in Writing Programme, under the direction of Adrian Frazier.

But by 2003, our little movement had stalled. Salmon Poetry had moved its headquarters from Galway years before. O'Ché's had closed. The Apostasy evenings petered out, and then Apostasy became Banana Phoblacht. In 2000, Galway's own Cuírt International Literary Festival had stopped running the event known as The Poets' Platform, in which unpublished local writers were invited to share a poem each. *The Cuírt Journal*, published by the Galway Arts Centre, stuttered to a halt at the end of the nineties amongst outcry; it was eventually replaced by *West 47*, a good magazine which nevertheless had an uphill battle to win trust amongst writers whose work had been misused by the *Journal* in its death throes.

Opportunities for emerging writers were drying up. There were many ideas to combat this – new magazines, writers' centres, readings series, websites. I remember many meetings, and then many launches as some of these ideas briefly took flight – only to be downed by lack of funds, lack of venues, or poor management.

It was frustrating. Here we were in Galway, a small city on the west coast of Ireland that had already given the world Salmon, Macnas and the Druid Theatre; three internationally recognised arts institutions. We had come here, we remained here, because we'd been promised another artistic flourishing. Of course, no individual had made any such promise. But we heard it anyway, in the rub of rain on stone. In the trad music that escaped like steam from the windows of the Crane Bar. In the echoes inside St. Nicholas Church. Local author Mike McCormack had published *Crowe's Requiem* (1998), a novel set in a youthful, Gothic, slightly mad Galway we recognised and embraced. There were many of us happy to stay up all night writing crazy modern masterpieces. But once we had written them, what then? I remember feeling that published authors existed on the other side of a pane of glass. I had no idea how to break the glass, to get through to where they were.

At the end of 2002, the writer and storyteller Rab Fulton (founder of "Muc Mhór Dhubh", a monthly mini-mag that celebrated multiculturalism and the arts) complained to me that no one was giving unpublished writers a chance to read – to practice the art of presenting work, to try out their pieces before an audience. Most of the readings advertised smelled either of new money or of old, mildewed worthiness. I thought about this lack a lot, and one winter's morning as I walked into town I decided I could see how to challenge it. I phoned Kevin; by the time I'd made it into work, he and I had created the format for the Over the Edge Readings.

In ten years, very little about the readings has changed. We've kept the project focussed by remembering its purpose; to provide a showcase for writers who've not yet published a book. Fifteen minutes for each of three readers (poetry or prose), followed by an open mic where absolutely anyone can get in on the act. It was discipline and joyful chaos walking hand in hand. The only modulation we've seen has been the increased ability of OTE to attract well-known authors as its popularity has spread. A tweak to the format resulted – we started putting one established writer on the bill with two unpublished. The juxtaposition upped everyone's game, and boosted the already high attendance as well.

From the start, our audience figures were healthy; we had indeed filled a need. These days, OTE commonly gets crowds of 50-75 people. There's no trick to this. At least one of our readers is always local, and is encouraged to bring every workmate and Great Uncle they've got. One reader is a name the literati will recognise. Lots of people come to do the open mic. And we publicise like mad – posters, emails, texts. Our shameless advertising and big crowds have raised eyebrows in some quarters. There will always be people who think that a literary experience is only any good if it's dull and poorly attended. Our audiences were recently taken to task in a national newspaper for being gauche enough to clap after every poem. Such unbridled enthusiasm makes some people nervous. These people should feel free to stay at home. OTE is not for them. We're for people who are new to writing and for those who are new to listening to writing as well. Kevin and I both teach writing classes now, for community colleges but also for schools, hospitals, rehab centres, retirement groups and people with disabilities. Students from these classes take part in OTE too, both as audience and talent. OTE greatly encourages the democratisation of literature by demonstrating the rich stew that results when everyone feels welcome to take part.

It was Kevin's stroke of genius to situate the readings in Galway City Library. We've had a wonderful working relationship with the library staff over the past decade. They tell us our presence has been beneficial to library services; if we've contributed half as much to the Library as the Library has to us, I'm happy. Every arts series needs a stable and welcoming home. Newcomers to OTE often mention that they felt comfortable attending their first literary event in a library, whereas a crowded bar or stuffy auditorium would've put them off.

As for hosts, the original plan was for Kevin and me to alternate. But I did the first one, and after that Kevin insisted I was the better person for the job. In ten years I've only missed one Over the Edge. I don't think I'm a natural public speaker; I'm shy, introverted, and in the early years had a very hard time with nervousness before the readings. I think I'm a good host for OTE because my own anxiety helps me tune in to the anxieties of readers. I treat them just as I would want a host to treat me. The crowd also senses this welcoming vibe and are relaxed by it too. There is an art to surfing the waves of enthusiasm generated by an audience. I've slowly learned that art, and I try to encourage our readers in that direction too. It involves trust. My job is to create a space where mutual trust can happen.

Over three hundred writers have read at OTE. About two hundred were unpublished at the time. Over forty of these have published books since, so that's roughly one in five of our up-and-comers. The vast majority of these are poets – proof that it's easier to publish a poetry collection than a book of short stories or a novel. In the past few years small presses, websites and magazines have begun to redress that imbalance by publishing more fiction. However, for most of the past ten years, OTE has been the only reading series in Ireland to include fiction writers alongside poets. Finally our lead is being followed, and fiction writers are stepping up to the mic in ever increasing numbers.

Half of our emerging writers who went on to be published had studied writing. OTE can be seen as both a cause and an effect of the recent boom in creative writing classes. As teachers, Kevin and I make an effort to bring writing students to OTE – ours, and others', including those doing the MA in Writing at the local university. I am never surprised to see past students succeed. Writers who seek out instruction; exposure to different methods; the energy and feedback of a classroom community, are writers who aren't precious about their product. They seek challenge, not praise. These writers are naturally going to rise to the top of our competitive profession.

OTE has worked to demystify the process of publication. The local fields are no longer full of writers waiting to be struck by lightning. Through the readings we've cleared a sort of path; take classes, do open mics, submit to journals, assemble a manuscript. There's more sense of a progression. This does not help everyone. Occasionally, ambitious writers mistake the path for a career ladder. They're crushed not to be Vice President of Haiku in the allotted five years. This is a mistake of ambition. Good writers are ambitious for their work, not for themselves.

For this anthology, I've assembled work by forty seven poets and fiction writers who published their first books after having read for Over the Edge. This book is a snapshot only; a glimpse at some of the work OTE has helped nurture. We're proud of these pieces, but then we're proud of all the writers with whom we have worked, whether they have published books or not. They have each taken a risk, each shared a bit of themselves with an audience, and we're happy to have been a part of that process.

It should of course be remembered that published writers take risks when they read as well. We were a long time persuading Rita Ann Higgins to read for us, as she feels nervous when onstage in her hometown. Michael D. Higgins, now Ireland's President, shook with nerves when reading his poetry at OTE. Michael Gorman commandeered an office in the library and spent nearly an hour sequestered, polishing his performance, before emerging to give a reading that looked off-the-cuff, unrehearsed. Joan McBreen read accompanied by music, which made us nervous, as it meant finding suitable equipment – I don't think we'd even got a microphone by then. The crime writer Ken Bruen also did something risky in his reading – he spent his fifteen minutes sharing his poetry, to the delight of our audience. Medbh McGuckian was one of our most gracious readers, and I'm still grateful for her supportive words to me when I was still struggling to find a publisher. More recently, Harry Clifton and Thomas McCarthy have given great performances at OTE, and been particularly pleasant company in the pub afterward. And the late Dennis O'Driscoll took an easy, unforced interest in the work of every writer he met at OTE, fledgling or established. It's a risk of a sort, to be so open to people and not forget how it feels to be, as it were, on the other side of the glass. It makes me happy to think how many of these warm encounters, between very successful writers and those just starting out, have happened at Over the Edge.

Then again, sometimes the risk lies in coming to the west of Ireland in the first place. The celebrated fiction writer Claire Kilroy is one of only two writers (so far) who have missed their own OTE reading (the other is Phil Abbink, who missed his in 2012 in order to be present at the birth of his son). Claire had tried to travel to us by train from Dublin, and got caught in the floods of November, 2009. Her texts to me were funny/scary: *the water is up to the windows...the track is flooded, they're putting us on a bus...we're circling the town, no way in...*She arrived in Galway some four hours later than scheduled, far too late to read, and spent most of the next day trying to find a way to go home. (We rescheduled with Claire, and her eventual reading was great.)

To fill the time that November evening, Kevin used a library computer to print out a few of his own poems and shared those with the crowd. This was one of only two times that Kevin has shared his own work at an Over the Edge. The other occasion was a few days before Kevin's mother died of lung cancer; he read a poem for her at the open mic. My own work has never been featured at an OTE, and never will be. I think this is one of the reasons the readings have lasted so long; we simply do not use it to promote our own work as writers. I've watched other arts ventures collapse because they turned into vanity projects for a small group of people. We avoid this by not featuring ourselves, and never having anyone else as a featured reader twice. This is why you hear writers refer to "my Over the Edge". You only get one. So it becomes a real marker, a singular moment in a career.

It's hard for me to believe we've now held over one hundred OTE readings. So much has happened in our lives over those ten years – we've gotten married, published four books apiece, travelled and given readings in many far-flung places. We've left the wood panelled apartment behind. We've also suffered financial setbacks, health setbacks, seen off threats to our work from various sources, and experienced great loss. Some months it has been hard to paste on our smiles and keep the show on the road. But that's the job.

I believe, though, that Over the Edge has also helped Kevin and me through tough times. There is something about both the ritualistic and communal nature of the readings that soothes, reassures. Am I straining for a metaphor if I liken the effect to that of church? Some will no doubt say I am. Yet how often have I seen that simple sound of a human voice, sharing a human experience in stirring language, lift and inspire an OTE audience? Lift and inspire me?

The careers of our readers have expanded in many directions, and so has Over the Edge itself. Our interests have led us down some pretty fruitful and fun paths. OTE now sponsors several Friday night writers' gatherings a year in addition to the original readings (which are always on Thursdays). Among these is a yearly Fiction Slam (the first in the country), and a yearly Poetry Book Showcase in which all local poets who have published a book in the past year are asked to come and share a few poems. We also organise the Westside

Open Mic, part of the Westside Arts Festival, every summer. And in 2012 we held the first annual Away With Words Over the Edge, specifically to showcase the writings of adults with intellectual disabilities. We have put together evenings highlighting Japanese and Polish poetry (led by the Polish and Japanese people in our community). In 2005 we helped organise a fundraiser for victims of the Indian Ocean Tsunami. In 2008, we joined Amnesty Ireland in staging a reading highlighting poetry by inmates at Guantanamo. And this year we have joined forces with Galway Pro-Choice to organise a reading in support of their work. We also run a writing competition, the Over the Edge New Writer of the Year, which brings in needed funds and helps us locate and support emerging writers throughout Ireland, and the world. I have included work by the two 2012 winners, Fiona Smith and Seán Kenny, at the end of this book.

In 2006, Maura Kennedy, then the Director of the Cuírt Festival, invited Kevin and myself to stage an Over the Edge Showcase as part of Cuírt. The Showcase features OTE readers chosen by the Cuírt Committee; it has remained a part of the Cuírt Festival programme. It is with a special pride and pleasure that I lead our unpublished OTE readers onto the Main Stage of Galway's Town Hall Theatre, where, thirteen years ago now, I nervously read a poem as part of the Poets' Platform.

Recently, a new poetry magazine called *Skylight 47* has emerged in Galway (the name an homage to the Arts Centre and the earlier *West 47*). OTE provides financial and creative support to the publication, which has an independent editorship. Among the elements setting *Skylight 47* apart from other journals – it carries reviews, editorials, in-depth interviews with poets. It's a magazine that talks back, that insists on a dialogue with modern poetry. This idea of literary appreciation as an interactive process is part of the ethos of OTE and, I hope, its most lasting legacy. At its best, Over the Edge expands people's vision of both literature and themselves. It encourages them to do a little work and gain the world of words.

More or less what we had in mind ten years ago, when we stood on our couch to see the sea.

# Learning to Cast

As with instruments in brass,
where getting the breathing right precedes
any catch of correct notes in the sky,
so your hours of hands-on lessons
in the fishing rod's unpunctual physics
and aping Maelzel's metronome
will all come long before anything
you'd call conjuring up a salmon's diet.

Because knowledge never happened by accident.

You'll spend all your fishless mornings
in an open field ignoring nearby rivers.
Sunsets peppered with midges will go by
conducting nature music until
you're sick of it before you have dry flies
get down to imitating real insects,
before whipping the air that hangs
over water vanishing past into
a believable feast and backing out
with your deceived dinner on a long leash.

*Umm ... alright*

*Love it.*

# Her and that Wardrobe

At first glance that wardrobe was good for firewood,
for the havoc of a quick hammering
in the yard below and best burned by Christmas.
What had you there but a pair of run-down doors
to hide the old outfits, a bottom so
*nice*  Swiss-cheesed in woodworm it could hardly
keep a drawer off the floor, a heap
of neglect then against the bedroom wall?

But when taken in hand it was not that.
When rubbed down with a steaming cloth
it started to tell of something else.
A few worm-plundered planks replaced,
dry joints rooted out for squeezing in new glue
and a pair of handles would set it off again.
So you took it outside on a fine day
in August, chisels hard ablaze
and the blade of a saw kept warm all day,
soaked in preserver stray wormholes turned fumaroles.

That evening it was back in its corner,
stinking of a workover, with all
the signs of the years you'd added on.
Or was it those it now claimed back?
Her Saturday readying herself in
its glass, a door open to shuffle through
and choose one dress for two, find the earrings
to go with, swinging to time as if time meant
forever. The drawer always slightly open,
the flash and frill of unmentionables.    *nice*

And won't you return here in a year
to see the ass fallen from another drawer?
Won't you come back to take out tools
and attempt the impossible,
start speaking from the hands again,
your dumb language wanting to promise everything?

oh...
when
did
that just
go?

Take an object +
describe it.

# Mary Ferriter
*RIP 1970*

She had no time for Santy;
why fool the children
when life is more like eating raw rhubarb
dipped in brown sugar,
from cones of rolled newspaper.

We squelched meal through our fingers
then scattered it.
Once we helped her chase a hen,
to send it to sleep,
head under wing.

She twisted its neck,
chuckled at our alarm,
then drew us in
to the wonder of it.

As she plucked it from her lap,
a halo of feathers about her white head,
we were given one severed leg each;
pull one cord to open,
another to close,
each waxen claw.

Soon we learned to enjoy
smashing dead fishes eyes with rocks,
watching the mercury discs spill out magic,
imagining what thoughts came
from their walnut-shaped brains.

When a calf died,
she opened it
to find the plug of mucus in its lungs,
the ball of hair in it's stomach,
or nothing at all astray.

Her advice to my mother on children;
*Bí ceannúil orthu,*
*Ach coimeád id chroí istigh é.*
Be fond of them,
but keep it safe inside your heart.

She forgot they see in.

Beautiful.

# Moonless

As a blind woman listens to the choir
she fingers her bracelet like rosary beads

pressing the gemstones between thumb and ring finger
then rolling them to middle and index

like rubbing butter into flour
to make coarse crumbs.

What do her fingertips divine
from the indentations and crevices?

Do they sense that black
has less heat to give, white more?

Her eyes blink and wash clean the surface
light passes through

light that never finds its way
to her seeing brain

never reaches her moonless consciousness
where chant and fingertip sensations frolic.

*oof*

## Today (extract)

Today starts off like this.

A man walks into the coffee shop, well-dressed, bearded, bespectacled, newspaper under his arm, and he appears normal, even gregarious: 'Geez it's warm in here,' is what he says. And Dara – and Dara is twenty-nine, ginger dreads, lumberjack shirt, red Yo-Yo Beans apron, today in charge of both the coffee shop and Claire, his thirteen-year-old sister, who is for reasons unknown to him lurking in the back staffroom, when by rights she should be at school – Dara gives a nervous laugh and says, 'Oh yeah man, I suppose it's fairly cosy alright.'

And he, the bearded man, says, 'Do you have the heat going? Full blast?'

Now this is a warning sign, if anyone's counting – but today, more than other days, is about picking battles. So Dara just shrugs, and agrees that he does (dude, it's December? It took me twenty minutes to de-ice my bike this morning?), and he opens his mouth to take the man's order but the man sighs, a long rush of ashtray breath in Dara's face, and he studies the coffee menu chalked up by the counter, and,

'I'll take a hazelnut cappuccino,' is what he says.

'One hazelnut cappuccino. No prob – '

'Geez it's warm in here.'

'I can turn down the –'

'Hah? It's very warm. Hah? *Crazy* warm. That's all I'm saying.'

Dara looks around. It's two weeks before Christmas. It's minus-five degrees outside. Nobody else in the café looks particularly crazy-warm – just swaddled and grateful, like they're so happy Yo-Yo Beans is open they could cry. The city is festively treacherous, compacted snow on the pavements and the canal in the process of crusting over. Half of its businesses will stay shut today, and Dara feels stung by this: this accusation from the public of bad service. He reaches up and makes a big show of turning down the heat. He'll turn it straight back up the second this guy leaves.

Actually, Dara had been feeling pretty good about his morning so far. Since he unlocked the doors at half past seven, Dara's handled nine breakfasts, he hasn't burnt a single bagel, and Abbie (his girlfriend, manager of Yo-Yo Beans) isn't even here to stand over him and make sure he gets it right. His lattes and macchiatos have been looking suspiciously good – as good as Abbie's, even; way better than Claire's. Dara's even been moving his butt a little bit to the Christina Aguilera Christmas album that's been playing on a loop on the shop stereo. He's been quick off the mark today: he's juggled take-aways and sit-ins, he's clocked up the tips and re-strung the tinsel, he's added free cinnamon biscuits to every order. He's been feeling – and this is not a word Dara would use lightly – *merry*.

So Dara delivers the cappuccino – and it's a perfect little thing of blown-silk milk and sweet fine dark powder – to his customer's table and without looking up the man flings aside his newspaper and says 'IT IS STILL TOO WARM IN HERE WILL YOU TURN DOWN THAT FUCKIN' HEAT.'

'I did turn down the heat, man!'

'You didn't turn it down *enough*. I was watching you. I saw that you only turned it down a couple of notches. What kind of place are you running here, anyway?'

Dara stands very still. At the top of the shop, Claire has come out from the staffroom and is hanging over the counter, looking like she's just wandered off the set of a 90s teen sitcom – *Saved by the Bell*, maybe, or *The Fresh Prince* – backwards baseball cap, a SWIM IRELAND T-shirt, leggings, hi-top Converse. Oh no he di'in't! Claire is mouthing. Oh no he did not!

Dara says, 'Right.' He heads back to the counter and looks at Claire and silently holds out his hand, and Claire passes him an empty takeaway cup, and now see him marching back down the aisle, Dara, ginger dreads bristling, see him pick up the china cup. See him slosh a hazelnut cappuccino into a paper beaker, and, 'Fuck off, so,' to the bearded man, see him say.

'Dara went nuts again and kicked out another customer,' Claire says, the second Abbie comes in at ten o'clock. Abbie is twenty-six, carrying a crate of milk, wrapped up in leather boots and a wool poncho and some borrowed real fur, already late, doesn't care for thirteen-year-old squealing – 'Is it too warm in here?' Abbie says. Abbie puts down the crate and straightens up, lets drop her fur, unzips her boots, steps into the black ballet shoes she wears when she is working. She checks her pockets for a tie for her hair, finds elastic bands, a pack of cigarettes. She flicks one of the elastic bands at Claire.

'OW, Abbie, don't *do* that!'

'Well, don't squeal on your brother, then.'

'Ow, Abbie...'

'And do your homework,' Abbie says. 'Do it and I'll make you a babycino.'

'Why, because I'm a baby?' Claire skulks back into the staffroom.

Abbie hunkers down and starts loading the milk into the fridge below the counter. Then she cleans the espresso machine, which is messy, and the workspaces around it, which are messy also, stained with pools of thickening milk, speckled with coffee granules. All of the things that need to be done, cleaned, sorted, prepared, and all of the figures, accounts, ingredients, stocklists, supplier-quantities, and invoice numbers, are stored in Abbie's head and in her body, in muscle memory, in various different brain-chambers, coded into her. Dara is co-signatory on their lease, but only Abbie has access to this particular master-list, though a list implies a sort of vertical arrangement, and that is not what it is at all: the things that must be done are spread wide in the air, here, there and everywhere, and Abbie spends her days spinning first this one, then the next, towards her, working upon them a  moment and then sending them out again, these glowing orbs, these gleaming dream-slides, and nothing ever quite *finished*, always an update to be done.

'Here, Abbie?' Claire's head has appeared around the wall. 'Just wondering, you know if you're putting marshmallows in the babycino? Can you put in two of the little ones instead of one of the big ones?'

'Go away, Claire,' Abbie says.

And Abbie is sick of it, sick of the master-list, sick of the city, Christmas, the Big Freeze, the crusted-over canal, the cheeky students, the begging dogs, the onion smells that rise at her in clouds when she opens the refrigerated cabinets to clean them. She is also sick of Claire; and when she realises that it is only half past ten and not half past four – God it is so dark today – and that consequently there is no reason for Claire to be here at this particular hour, Claire's school being one of the few in the city that has stayed open throughout the bad weather – Abbie bursts open the staffroom door.

Inside, Claire is starfished on a beanbag, an open maths book on her stomach like a broken bird. Claire 'I-can't-I-have-my-period' DeLacey; Claire who lifts her head and says it now, her refrain, blinking with piteous eyes across to where Abbie stands at the door, index finger still locked on the switch. Claire chants it through a mouthful of the olive hair she keeps twined in a plait, the end of which she sucks industriously: I have my period, Claire says, and Abbie bends and shoves Claire's schoolbag and swim kit from her path, straightens, and flips the light switch on and off. On/off, goes Abbie's finger, on/off, Claire why are you sitting here in the darkness?

'Because I like the darkness,' Claire says.

In the staff toilet, Abbie shimmies her bum into black stretchy work pants. Abbie paints Chapstick on her mouth. She looks at the pedal bin, which is overflowing with green and purple wrappers and wads of tissues, and which reeks: of blood, of sweet rotting flowers, of something that should be kept away from dogs and men. On her way back out, Abbie smacks the calendar on the wall: dust shivers from the month of December.

Claire stares her down with olive eyes. 'It's the canal,' Claire says. 'It brings it on.'

'The *canal* brings on your period. Twice a month?'

'The canal,' says Claire, waving her hand, 'the full moon, the ice-tides...'

Abbie, binding herself into a red Yo-Yo Beans apron, says, 'If all the women of the world just opted out of life when they had their periods, what would happen?'

Claire shouts, from the depths of her chest, 'YOU'RE NOT TAKING ME SERIOUSLY YOU DON'T UNDERSTAND HOW BAD I FEEL'. She scrunches her body further into the beanbag and pulls up her knees. She begins to weep: the tiny, heartbreaking sounds of an ancient grief. She clamps the maths book over her head and cries into it. Abbie checks the CCTV. A man has come in, is standing by the door, looking around.

*

The man's name is Conor Doherty. He is partially deaf. He wears real sapphires in his ears. He has lion-blond hair and lion-blond eyelashes. He is looking for Claire DeLacey, who has not, for reasons menstrual, shown up for her school's swim training this morning. When Abbie comes out front, face primed with hellos, he is waiting, standing against the counter, helping himself to a day-old muffin, picking the bun apart with his fingers. As ever, he has that air of holiness about him, that... essence of bishop, artless, unmovable, a man of great and patient ambition. Sometimes when Abbie meets him she is struck by the thought that he would like her to kiss them, the sapphires, and some day too she will do it. Some day, she will lean across the counter and tip a sinner-kiss onto each of those gemstones – but for now, they began to sign to each other, a trick that Abbie, over the last three years, has become proficient at.

They sign, flashing their fingers, and, as always in the Yo-Yo Beans by the canal, the windows sputter with weird green shadows, and the smell of the canal seeps in. In the Yo-Yo Beans by the canal, the sofas are threadbare, and the display cabinet – for sweet cakes and slices – is too small. The menu is mendacious. The muffin that Conor is eating has been baked offsite, is pumped full of hydrogenated vegetable oil, contains additives that are a known cause of cancer – but Abbie is cute: cute like a barmaid spirited up out of the last century, cute like she's got other plans cooking, cute like she's long understood when not to comment. 'Haven't seen her, Conor,' Abbie says. 'Not a clue.''

ALAN McMONAGLE

# Bloomsday Bus Driver

When I was a young lad the sun used to shine all day on the sixteenth of June. Up it came at ten to five in the morning and didn't disappear until twenty past ten that night. We lived five miles from the sea and one Bloomsday morning my mother gave me a pound and said, 'Off with you now, go get a tan and figure out your life'. So I made my way to the station, gave the pound to the bus driver, sat in behind him and stared out at the clear blue sky.

The thing was everybody knew about the sun coming out on the sixteenth of June, and so the bus had to stop every twenty-five feet or so to pick up another passenger bound for the shimmering waters. By my steadily improving mathematical calculations that meant the bus was going to stop more than a thousand times before reaching the sea. I was glad I had inherited my father's knack for patience.

To help distract everyone from the start-stop nature of the journey the bus driver provided a running commentary. 'It's a great day to be alive,' he said as people clambered aboard. 'I wish I had the day off myself,' he offered as he punched holes in tickets. 'You are lucky, lucky people,' he declared as he eased the bus back into motion.

About four hours into our journey, with over half of the five-mile trip already behind us, the driver stopped the bus even though nobody had flagged it down.

'I'll be back in a second,' he said, climbing out of his seat. 'I want to ask that foxy lady a question.'

She was leaning against a wall, licking an ice-cream cone. Some ice-cream was smeared across her top lip. She was wearing a white dress, and every few seconds some wind reached in off the close-by sea and lifted the dress a few inches above her knees. The bus driver leaned against the wall beside her. He plucked a long stem of reed-grass and started chewing on it. After a moment he pointed to the ice-cream cone. The lady passed it over, and he ditched his reed and took a gob-full. When the ice-cream was gone the lady jerked a thumb over her shoulder. Then the two of them disappeared inside the house set back off the road. We all stared out to see what was happening. Some passengers became worried.

'I need to get some sun today,' said one fretful lady. 'I'll die if I don't.'

'Yes, but how are we going to get to the beach?' said another. 'That lad is very distracted.'

'Does anyone know how to drive a bus?'

I wished I could've said, 'I do'.

Instead, one or two older men took it upon themselves to replace the absent bus driver. They strode purposefully through the aisle of the bus, one with a poor excuse for a moustache growing above his lip, the other wearing a straw hat and a jacket with stripes. The man trying to grow a moustache winked as he passed the worried ladies, as if to say, don't panic girls, I'll have us on the way to the sun in a jiffy. But when he and his accomplice reached the driver's seat they realised the bus man had taken the keys with him. At once they threw their arms into the air, turned to their expectant crew members with a look of helplessness and the fretting started all over again.

'Look,' someone to the back of the bus spoke out, with traces of fear entering his voice. 'The sun is starting to go down.'

'I'm going to die,' the fretful lady said. 'I really am.'

There wasn't much talking after that. Everyone sat back into their seat, sighing at the fading sun and at the sombre shadow gradually enveloping the countryside. Then we spotted the bus driver. He was rushing down the pathway of the house he had been inside, tugging his shirt back into his half-way-down trousers. His hair was tossed and one of his shoes was missing. As soon as he climbed into his seat he was in no mood to hang about.

'I'll drive you all home personally,' he said, and one or two women raised their eyebrows.

'That was one reluctant bus driver,' said the lady who thought she was going to die when we pulled up at my stop.

'Young lad,' he said as I stepped off, and he flipped a coin at me. At once I made a dash for Mel Campbell's paper shop, he always stayed open late.

'I'll have an ice-cream cone,' I said to the girl behind the counter. 'One with a flake in it.'

She took a cone from the stack beside the ice-cream machine, pulled the lever and, once she could pile on no more, offered me the towering sculpture along with a smile that, in times to come, would make the wind blow across my soul. It was more or less dark when I stepped inside the kitchen of our house.

'That's not much of a tan,' my mother said when she looked up from her paper.

'No,' I agreed, 'but when I'm big I'm going to be a bus driver.'

## Slum Pottery   *Love it*

Hello everybottle.
I do ippiligise
Because at the moment
I seem to be surfing from a rare contradiction
Leaving me willfully unable to pronouns my werbs probly.
It's obviously a dammaged nerve correction between my monde
and my vice,
So consequently my speak patter is up fuct
And all my weirds come outwrung.
Now...
I find this condition particularly embracing
Because I was starting to be thit of
As a pot of a curtain amount of skull
(whither I am a skullful pot or not is, of kiss, open to de boot.)
However,
Recently I was licky enough
To be the whinger of a Slum Pottery computation.
And since then I've knitted that
There's been a lot written and sad about Slum Pottery.
*What is* Slum Pottery?
Is it a farm of hamster rap?
Is it wit man's hop hip?
What is Slum Pottery?
Well, as far as I can sue,
Slum Pottery is a pitiful camp expression
Where mumbles of the undience are randomly secreted
And asked to give scores to the various potters on stage.
The potters get up, see their poms
And at the end of the note,
The potter with the heightest score wines.

But is it fair?
Is it judged on the pom or the perferation?
(It's a difficile question)
Should worms be spooky
Or should worms be red from the platter?
And what if the potter, like me,
Has trouble seeing his poms correctly...
Keeps seeing his poms wrangly...
Or indeed...
Gets his wrong in the words order.
Will the undience take the pass out of him for being sally?
At the very lost,
It would put the potter at a serious damp inventage.
No.
I think it's about trime
We were all a bit more syphilitic
And embrace all sins of pittery and pottery.
After all,
What makes one pom gad and one pom bud?
It's an age old pizzling condom run.
Well,
Time wanes for no one.
So it's probably beast if I retarded from the stooge to let you
make up your own moons.
Thank you very much.
And I hope you licked my pom.

# Avalanche

When the avalanche came down on us

it did not come down on us in a holy light,
flickering between this dimension and another

ultraviolet one. It did not shower its sermon upon us
in meaning-ful, vowel-less sounds like stalactites.
It did not come down on us at all. It came up, up, over

and around us; all around us in a pall. It met our bodies
in a hail, hail, hail, not a wall but heavier than water
if we were sitting at the bottom of the sea. We heard it crack
and sizzle on the ground. It filled the valley like a steam engine;

its clotted vapour urging forward to some terminus beyond us.
We watched it soar and could not inhale enough air between
the screams. Our lungs made fists. I thought of lips freezing shut
once and for all, the uncommon cold, no human fingers to close
the lids nor chance of rescuing the bodies, stiff as candy canes

striped red, white, red, white, grey. Your hands were fifty feet away,
your mind another hundred. My cries could not contend with this parade
of physics. You were wordless, as if the snow were slow motion surf
or a weir devouring its atmosphere. Was it fluid dynamics, glaciology
or meteorology you surveyed? There was something of the shock
wave about it, no doubt about that. The space between us

prolonged. I should never have collapsed in love with a physicist.
I saw the fort my brother built from bales of hay, whose tunnel
should never have been trusted. Oh, to make a hay citadel!
'When the fields are white with daisies,' my father would have said.
The ice wave rose and darkness fell. I doubted how well my elbows

would act as pick-axes, if it were to be a catacomb. I had once been told
that knowing which way is up is key: that the whiteness is homogenous;
that people dig madly, burying themselves in the immortal white. I panicked:
would he have a better chance than I, with his gall; his practicality?
No, the snow was nothing like confetti. It would not applaud any small boys
or any small girls, no matter how insolent. We braced ourselves, finally.

Later, you described the form of a loose snow avalanche as a teardrop;
borne of some great disparity between the tensile gift of snow layers
and their compressive heft. The angle of repose was soft, you allowed,
as we stood in the catchment area, making observations and vowels sounds.

## I Dream in Solid Pine

The bed divides us. We take sides,
mine piled book-high with
balms, night creams, a clock.
His with books, a light, a digital clock.

We meet lustily in the middle,
then sated, roll back where we
came from. No place for sound
words between the posts.

The bed is solid, framed in pine.
It passed the shake test
the day we bought it, tired
as always, in a hurry.

The third bed in our history –
also the longest drop to the floor.

like it

Nice

# Brigit (the Accidental Bishop)

Sometimes men do these things, you know.
Forget themselves, lose the run of themselves,
forget that they're supposed to treat women differently
and next thing you know, you've been made a bishop
underneath your wimple and shaved head.


Except you're not allowed to do the day-to-day
rituals because you're a woman –
the sacraments of marriage or birth or death –
so they have to kit you out with a team
of driver-priests to cart you around the country,
baptise the babies for you,
wed the men and women, accompany death.


Everywhere you go, the women greet you
with empty butter churns, casks of water,
sick children and mothers.
You belong to them, and the small tricks
you picked up along the way –
foxglove for fever, Guelder-rose for birth pangs,
a spare bladder of cream in your bag –


spread like folklore up and down the country
until the whispers turn into your name
and the women have claimed you:
poetry under your breath, fire shooting
above your head, mistakes and all.

## Fearless

*Love it*

Fearless
I'm fuckin fearless
Try me now why don't ya
An' I promise ya faithfully
Ya won't last too long

Cos I'm the wan they're all on about
When they're drinkin their fuckin coffee
Above in Sullivan's café
Yeh I'm the wan that ripped the fag machine
Down off the wall above in Bernie's lounge

I'm the likes that spreads myself out on a bench
Above in the square of a summer's day
Suckin a flagon with me shirt tore off an' me pot belly out
Fuckin an' blindin anywan who'd be passin
Tellin dem I'm fearless fuckin fearless

Last Friday I got shteamed above in Cork
Got fucked outta Henry's for bitin some youngfella's ear off
Well as I was passin out beyond the viaduct
I got a mad tashpie to run out on the road
An' I screamin into the headlights how I'm fearless fuckin fearless

I'm the laziest oul bollox that ever you met
But I'd ate your fuckin eyeballs in a shot
I 'm barred from every pub in town an' every bookies too
But I'd walk to Tipperary for a drink an' a bet
Yeh I'd walk to Tipperary for a drink an a bet

Cos I'm fearless
Fuckin fearless
Don't believe me?
Doubt me now?
Watch me go so.

Till I stick a pint glass into me brow
An' lepp up onto the counter like a pure fuckin tiger
An' kick the heads wan by wan off the beer taps
And I watchin meself in the big bar mirror
As I dance in the blood an' the fountains o' beer
Yeh as I dance in the blood an' the fountains o' beer

# Instructions for Following a Priest

The priest must be very old, at least one hundred years old.
Following a priest of that age is difficult.
One must have great patience and even greater guile.
You must not break pace and come too near behind
as he shuffles along slow and halting and afflicted and miserable
like the middle ages.
You must maintain at least the distance of his shadow
in the noonday sun. Otherwise he may feel or even smell your
    breath, and turnaround
or cry for assistance.
The priest must not be allowed to sense that he is being followed.
But, what are the senses of hundred year old?
Not much more surely than the senses of a biscuit or a peat briquette?
Wrong. The elderly lose some senses but they
gain others. The priest may 'hear' you through the tremors
going up through the soles of his feet. Because of this it is always better
to follow the priest near flowing traffic, in the ambit of large
    construction projects,
or close by volcanoes. So that your footsteps and potential other
vibrations are indistinguishable. Personally I prefer the highlands of
    Borneo,
footpaths of the inner ring road of Madrid, or practically anywhere
    in Dubai
as great priest-following locations. But there are plenty others.
    Use your imagination.
If you can't guess the secret places priests will go you have no
    business trying to follow them.
Anyway, not rousing the suspicion of the priest is one thing
but not rousing the suspicion of onlookers is at quite another
    level of difficulty.
Doing anything suspicious in the direction of the elderly,
perhaps especially elderly in religious habits, can draw rapid,
    vengeful native intervention

on you. But there is a way out of this, one that I have personally developed to perfection

over years and years of priest following. This is to make like you are

following the priest in some official capacity, as his lay assistant, or as a younger priest.

You can pretend to be saying the rosary or something. You can even carry a large crucifix

or a fake chalice if you like. After a while a rhythm will develop. Your footsteps, your

breathing and your heartbeat will match exactly that of the priest. This is the nirvana point.

Or plateau, if you can make it last. But don't forget how slow the priest is and how little he

needs to eat. You will have to break off for refreshment at some point. Most importantly,

do not dress up as one hundred year old priest. You know well what will happen if you do.

# Peace Fire

The Halloween visit has become a ritual,
the car laden with excited children,
dillisk, mussels and salmon
fresh from the Atlantic,
and copies of *The Western People*.
Such joy at reunion, Bridge partners,
North and South.
and the welcoming aroma, so distinct,
of hot 'purdy' pudding,
steaming, spicy and swimming in melted butter.

Relax now, the journey's over and Hurray!
We're in time for *Coronation Street*.
We laugh at David Hanly's slip of the tongue,
"peacefire" he'd said on *Morning Ireland*.
Have things changed we ask, have you seen a difference?
Well, there's a picnic area now, at Boa Island,
Where once there was the camouflaged checkpoint.
You can eat you sandwiches now in the sun
wind, rain and spikes in the road consigned to memory.
Oh. And berets replace helmets
and the boy soldier waved
at the smiling boy who saw only *Action Man*.

 The black night sky erupts in myriad colours,
moonlight rainbows, explosions everywhere,
friendly fire of bangers, Catherine wheels
from the fireworks display in the fairground.
Children's voices ricochet,
gasps of astonishment
and screams of wonder
in awe of a primeval bonfire, spiralling.
Sparks beseech the heavens,
praying to ancient Gods
that this time the ceasefire holds.

# Tiananmen Square, 2002

No talk of tanks.
We're told they fly kites here, practice tai chi,
take pictures back-dropped with Forbidden City
and a hugely looming Chairman Mao.
Scammers swarm toward round-eyes like us.
Street-vending hoards, to which we're taught to say
*bu yao* –
*don't want* – sell fake Rolexes,
watches with waving Maos,

plastic Chinese flags, ice cream for children.
Our guide explains, "People from the country.
Blond hair, blue eyes new to them,"
as hundreds of hands fly to our children,
one line snaking toward my son, another, longer,
toward my daughter,
who waves her plastic flag,
Mao smirking over her shoulder,

caught by Chinese cameras for later release
in photo album fields.
One father proudly
places beside her a small sullen son,

who looks into the unfamiliar blue, and screams.

## Night Watchman *(extract)*

To say he kept himself to himself would be an understatement. He actively avoided human contact and this, curiously, did him no harm at all in his job. The opposite in fact. Over the years the manager would often say how useful it was to have a night watchman who had built up an air of mystery around himself, because whenever people talked about him it was usually in fearful tones. The Bright family were convinced their stock would never be robbed while Terence was on watch. They were right. But stock isn't the only thing to worry about.

Terence brought sandwiches and a flask to his hut at the gate, timing his arrival for just after the day workers had gone home. He would wait outside until the day security left only then entering the hut. He made his rounds three times nightly like clockwork. He liked to walk in the shadow. On his rounds he walked along the lines where the bulbs were assembled and packed, he walked through the offices, he saw how each worker organised their little space, a personal touch here or there, a snapshot of a loved one, a postcard of a sunny beach which gave an annual two weeks respite from the artificial lights of the factory floor. Without them knowing it Terence got to know a little bit about each person who worked there during the days. From the things they left and the way they left them he made them his friends, his family. He knew that Myke from the stores had a secret crush on Carry in accounts because of the newspaper clippings Myke kept stowed in his locker. Carry's basketball career was fanatically chronicled and followed by Myke. What Myke didn't know but Terence did was that Carry, although a newlywed, kept the anonymous Valentines card that Myke had snuck in early to leave on her seat. She kept it in the locked bottom drawer of her desk pedestal. Terence had a key to every lock. He knew that Mandy in personnel struggled with money and her weight, one a consequence of the other, a succession of yo-yo diets meaning she was frequently broke and even more frequently she shed quiet tears in the ladies. He knew that the HR manager kept a cell phone in his desk which he never brought home and that only one number ever used that phone. He never deleted any of the texts and sometimes liked to stay a little late to savour them. He knew that the stationery store could be locked from the inside and sometimes was used for more than storage. He knew what had gone on in there that day when he stood for a little while in the dark room and sniffed the air. He never let himself spend too long in there.

Although he rarely met any of them, over the years he began to think of them as his family. He was content that his impulses were under control, he had his family and he knew the things they allowed others to know and the things they allowed nobody to know. All in all his life went from hour to hour, day to day, week to week and year to year as he hoped it would. He walked the silent corridors by night, his family around him, got home in the early morning and slept from 9am until 4pm. Then he ate alone and walked in the park alone, careful to avoid people, in particular he steered clear of amorous couples and the playground. Once he had walked close to where the children were swinging and had been accosted by two mothers asking which one of the children belonged to him. He never went that way again.

One Autumn night Terence went on his rounds and decided to sit in an office for a few moments. He often did this and used to sit in the Human Resource managers desk and flick through the individual personnel files learning more about who was who and who was what. There was a manila file on the desk, unmarked. He opened it to find a small advertisement clipped from a newspaper for an efficiency consultant. Attached to the clipping were several CV's. He thought nothing of it. Friday evening, two weeks later Terence sat on the factory wall under the trees waiting for the daytime security to leave the hut. They took longer than usual and he was beginning to feel the dampness from the wall creep up his backbone when the door finally opened and Fred lumbered to his old car. He was shaking his head as the springs complained when he sat in. Terence walked past with a quick wave but was pulled up short by a holler from Fred.

"Batty..hey hold up a sec." He puffed as he rolled down the window.

Terence walked over but didn't look up.

"You're going to have fun this evening, you ought to see what they got lined up for you my friend." Beads of sweat rolled down his face as he spoke.

"Came in this morning and it was all change. Seems the big wigs want us to be more professional, so they got someone to whip us into shape. I got to lose twenty pounds if I want to keep my job, can you believe it?"

Terence stared into the car and realised that this was the most conversation he had ever had with Fred. The floor inside was peppered with fast food wrappings and cigarette ends. He looked at the car as it drove off. It seemed to tilt a little on the driver side. Terence walked into the security hut to be met by the HR manager and a woman. He stopped at the door, unsure whether to go in or not. The manager beckoned him in with a cursory wave of his hand. The woman had a small handbag perched on Terence's desk.

"Have a seat."

Terence went to sit down but seemed put off by the bag. He hesitated. She cottoned on immediately and moved it, at the same time flashing him a toothy smile and holding out her hand.

"I'm Grace."

He shook her hand and as he did her expression changed, she withdrew hers and when he looked away she wiped it on her skirt. Terence could feel the sweat begin to gather in his armpit.

"Right Terence, Grace is here to study how we do things and to see if we can all do them a little better, time and motion studies that kind of thing."

He sounded enthusiastic but then management always did about the things they hoped wouldn't affect them directly.

"So, she's going to be spending a little time looking at the way each of us do our jobs and then give us pointers on how we could do better."

Grace crossed her legs and even with his eyes glued to the floor Terence knew she had sheer nylon tights covering shapely legs. He twisted to look out the window. The stragglers from the day shift drifted out through the gates, laughing and playacting, most of them already ready for a Friday night out. He looked back at the floor. His heart felt like it was trying to escape from his chest.

The manager got up.

"Right I'll let you have a little chat."

Terence almost got up and left with him, for a second he felt trapped, alone with this woman.

The door closed behind him before Terence could react.

"I'm glad he's gone." Grace unbuttoned her suit jacket and slung it over the chair.

"I know it seems intimidating but honest to God all I'm here to do is look at working methods and suggest efficiencies, I'm sure we'll get on fine you and me, now do you have a kettle here or am I going to have to go all the way to the canteen for a cup of tea?"

Terence got up and put the kettle on, her relaxed manner caught him off guard and he found himself unusually at ease.

He kept his back to her as he made the tea and couldn't remember the last time he had been alone with a woman apart from his mother. He focused his mind on the task at hand and that seemed to help.

"You can stop stirring now." Her voice had a hint of a laugh.

He turned back and for the first time looked at her as he handed her the steaming mug.

She sat cross legged, her skirt an inch above her knee. She was small, brown haired and her face was the shape of a heart. She pulled her skirt over her knee.

"Thanks, right next Wednesday I'll spend a few hours with you as you do your job, and we'll see where we go from there, is that alright?"

Terence nodded as she passed him back her mug.

"Ta ra so see you next week, relax we might even have fun, you never know." And she was gone.

Terence sat alone and smelled the air. He sat where she had and the seat was still warm from her. He sat there for a long time. He didn't go on any rounds that night. The next day he slept fitfully. When he walked in the park he walked past people without even noticing them.

That night he rushed in to work. He was sitting on his wall an hour before it was time for him to start. He counted crows to make the time pass. He was at two hundred and seventy three when Fred finally left. He noticed Fred doing a little jog to the car, his potbelly jiggling, maybe if he did that every day for the next thirty years he'd drop the requisite twenty pounds. Then he watched the light in the HR office through his hut window until it darkened. He waited for the manager to leave and then he went to his office. His breathing was shallow when he sat at the desk and opened the file.

Grace Goodyear, Management Consultant.

Born 1976.

The list of qualifications and experience stretched for three pages. He devoured the file in seconds and then went back to read slowly over it. By the time he was finished he knew by heart all that Grace wanted anyone to know about her. A passport photo was attached to the CV. He pocketed this. When he found himself imagining what their children would look like he slammed the pedestal drawer on his hand to regain some control. Nonetheless as he left the office he had a little smirk on his face. The next four days were the longest of his life.

## Tribe

When they found themselves on the new ground,
the tribe felt astray, like they had no right or claim
to be caught there. The marks and odours of the fond past
were absent, just a worrying plastered freshness
and an unhindered winter-chill breeze.

There were no signs of usual purpose,
labour on boats or barrels, no cooper's aprons,
no docker's haunts, granite steps, sawdust pubs,
no lorry-scutting, no animal gangs.
Blackened teeth were outlawed. A charwoman
was a 'cleaner' and corpses were laid out by nurses.
No smell of hops or putrid river, no tuggers,
fancy-women, kip houses, coal boats, stone bruises,
slop buckets.
Everything new was a form of no.
It was all to happen like a sink draining,
no questions asked, no answers given.
Go.

There were still and shady trees, and if no trees
there were fields, or 'meadows' as was said
in the new language. The suddenly original children
were to have childhoods, their own clean bed
raised on legs off the floor and no toil intended.
Books were forced in the new doors,
to be read and re-read. At times a studious quiet descended
that was never heard before, tight as a judge.
Soon there was a grammar imposed on breathing itself
on the raised voice and shiny accents, softer melodies
masking all the rough bliss that went before.

There were signs of livestock, dark forms,
stragglers, keeping shyly to the distance.
The tribe didn't know the names of these breeds,
neither had the animals seen the tribe's like,
and soon without ceremony or comment
the cattle and other beasts vanished
as the massed roofs pushed westwards,
trailing car-parks and shopping centres,
motorists,
customers.

ELAINE FEENEY

# Urban Myths and the Galway Girl

She tells us as we jump
about like idiots
it was so cold this morning she
thought the holocaust was upon her–
and she'd just failed her driving test
again
because she couldn't follow around a rear window,
shir that's a ridiculous thing to do
she'd be in the sea
because he'd brought her around
Ballyloughane
and that's no place to be.
She loves the way the globe is warming
loveeeeen
the heat is lovely.
She had a crush on the bus driver who took
the Castlelawn-Eyre-Square-Salthill
Skeff for a quick one route
but ended up with the TV man who came to
fix her father's Ferguson once a year.
he told her that this Christmas
she'd need to tart herself up

The Fat Bastard

But they've nice bling in River Island
so she'll tog out there
loveeeeen
even if he is a fat bastard
shir ya have to keep them happy.
But lately she muses,
she's gone off her husband,

he walks around the house in tracksuit pants
loveeeeeeen
with his sweaty limp bollicks hanging sideways,
'tis enough to turn a nun off'
but he's great for the painting
and cleaning out the ashes all the same.
she tells me the youngest with Autism is
growing out of it.
And again she tells me about the foreign national
who left the buggy at the bus stop
only this time she's set it in Salthill and not Mervue.

She's the queen of Urban Myths

She wishes she had a car and could get this five grand for the taxi
that the coloured lads are getting.
quote
unquote
she's saying 'coloured' because she knows
I'm a bit funny about racism.

She tells us about Jimmy her boss.
It's complicated she says
you have to let him think he's one up on ya
and then have one up on him
and you'll be one up–
I think
Then catch him out.

She's four stone loveeeen
she has an over active thyroid
an under-active husband
a touch of type two diabetes
an over-anxious daughter
the odd outbreak of psoriasis
a query of meningo-cockal-cock-something
and definite insanity

everywhere in Galway waters down her vodka.
She'll tell Pauline that Christine is a wench
she'll tell Christine that Pauline is loose.
She tells me about all the pills the husband is taking
for the cough and the limp dick and all
nothing is working
loveeeeen.
Now she couldn't care if he went in his sleep.

She's fond of the new pope but not the look of him
loveeeeen
Fond of roundabouts
loveeeeen
The twenty per cent off at Tesco's
loveeeeen
She thinks Billy on Eastenders did very well for himself
loveeeeen
But they should really drown that Gail from Corrie
loveeeeen
She's interested in organic veg the oddtime
loveeeeen
Read they were great for constipation
loveeeeen
Because she has piles like a bunch of grapes
and a box so itchy she could feck it out a window.

And finally she gives me a Six Star Plan
for the Perfect Me;
My nails would look great with false tips
My eyes with false lashes
My skin with fake bake
My teeth with fake bleach
My abdomen with fake liptrim
My vagina with a sneaky tuck.

But my boobs are grand,
grand altogether,
loveeeeen!

# Contact

I gaze for comets and omens,
all apparent in the night shapes,
the castles built on the clouds,
those ships that form the Armada,
which close in on the moon.

My eye captures the star
that is a thousand light years away,
omitting radiation, splitting particles,
filtering through history,
touching this unremitting daytime.

I spend my given hours
charting its course across the meridian,
convinced of its oceans,
its civilizations of knowledge
and vast continents of freedom.

But does it turn its powerful observatories on me,
mapping another presence in its cosmos,
realizing that all I am doing
is reflecting the death of cities.

## My Father's Lands *(extract)*

The beach lay in a narrow cove on the eastern side of the island. Ronan knew the terrain well. An assortment of hefty boulders guarded its sides and protected the island from storms. This was the only way in. Elsewhere submerged rocks would tear at their boats and they would not find a break in the granite wall big enough to anchor.

He steered carefully over the pebbled floor. On the beach a battered boat half full of water lay on its side. Ronan stiffened. "The fools."

The reference to the men who crossed before the storm jolted Finola. The Lord Deputy was in Derry. There was no need for alarm. Doubtless, they were harmless visitors. In the middle of a storm? She did not stop to examine the scuttled boat. She had to find her son.

Running along the beach, she reached the path to the centre of the island, all the time gulping in air. It was eerily silent. Morning, it was early and they were all asleep she told herself. The discarded boat had been there for weeks. The elements hadn't touched it although it was directly in the eye of the storm. Fooling herself with lies, she reached the island's living quarters, her lungs about to explode.

No clay and wattle houses greeted her. No golden buttercups decked the grasses. No colours of spring here. There were just hillocks of grey ashes, some small some bigger and all smoking. Ronan caught up with her, breathing heavily. They did not speak as they looked at the devastation. At every step, they expected to see people.

"The caves," she said. "When the Lord Deputy burned their houses, they would have gone for shelter in the caves." Her voice shook. "Who else could it have been but the Lord Deputy?" She looked at Ronan, her expression desperate.

"'Tis to break up we should," he said. "You take the near ones and I'll be taking the ones over there." He patted her shoulder. "God bless you."

She ran to the far edge of the island stumbling and tripping on the coarse knotty grass. "Andrew Óg. Where are you? Are you there Niall? Answer me." Her voice thin and high rang out in the silence. Each time she stumbled, she picked herself up again. She had fallen many times before she reached the first cave.

Ridged along the borderline, the caves were like little limestone houses. After the brightness, the half-darkness inside was a balm. She smelled the damp air and heard the sound of water trickling, the only noise. "Grandmother? Grandfather? Where is everybody?"

As she scrambled to the third cavern, she tripped over what seemed to be a human form. Horrified, she looked down. Her stomach somersaulted. Seamus had died in the act of fleeing. A ball to his back had killed him.

She heard Ronan calling to her and turned again to run to him. He must have found something.

"Don't go in," he said. He was standing at the mouth of the fourth cave. He shook his head. "'Twill do you no good."

She looked at him, not in confusion and horror, but in knowledge. "Andrew Óg?" she whispered in someone else's voice. "My son?"

He did not look at her. "Some are alive," he said. But she already knew the truth.

She entered the cave. Walked among the stalactites and stalagmites oddly beautiful against all this ugliness. She saw grandfather and grandmother sitting, staring. How dare they be alive when her son might be dead? They were old. And Niall. He had burns on his face. Blood streamed down his tunic. She turned away not wanting to see what he held in his arms. Later. She'd look later. She walked among the corpses. Some were alive among them. Three boys and two girls, with crazed eyes, clung to each other. She hugged each child in turn, touching their blisters with her lips.

She turned back to Niall. Having to know, she took the bundle from his arms. Andrew Óg's face looked unmarked, he had escaped the flames but not the thrust of a knife in the ribs. He was wearing his red tunic. His mouth hung open. She noticed that he had grown a new tooth since she last saw him.

Ronan rowed back to the mainland for reinforcements to clear the island of its dead and bring back the living. He rang the rusty bell in the church belfry. They came out of their houses, the women, the children and the old men. The husbands had gone fishing further up the coast, but were still within hailing distance.

The children skipped happily glad of an excuse to leave the confinement of the house. The old men sucked on their teeth, their faces resigned. The sea had claimed their loved ones before. The women gathered in groups, taking succour from each other. Relief mingled with compassion on their faces when they heard the news. None of their own had drowned this time. It was sad all the same.

Every available boat within miles of the island came. The water, now still after the storm, rippled from the onslaught of oars. Following in their wake, the seabirds seemed to sing a dirge. Nobody spoke as one by one the fishermen helped the wounded to the boats. They went where they were told, looking sporadically towards the open sea fearing another attack.

"I won't go without Andrew Óg. He can't go with the living," Finola whimpered. "I'll stay here."

Ellen gathered some kindling, took a flint from her pocket and managed to get a spark. Pursing her lips, she blew on it until it caught fire.

Finola was still shivering

Ellen squeezed her shoulder and settled to wait with her. Later that day Ronan returned for them. With her son in her arms, Finola sat in a trance in the curragh.

Three of Ellen's grandchildren, one of them a man of twenty two, rode to the Campbell fortress to tell them that their enemies had wiped out their clan. "'Twas when the storm quieted for a couple of hours yesterday they crossed. They returned in the early hours of the following morning."

An Irish chronicle recorded their deaths. It ended with the words:

*Upon a more pleasant isle the sun never shone. Pity to see it befouled by the caked blood and ashes of so many aged, children, women, babes … Herod left their bodies strewn on the grass. Ochón … ochón … bewail the slaughter of the innocent.*

# GERALDINE MITCHELL

## Lull

If I could walk into a painting
it would be this one. Slip
into silence and looking back
see your mouth moving,
let the glass hold me, the sun
unpack me pore by pore.

In here, no breath. No movement
over the green-washed fields
or the woods beyond.
No sound but the soft hiss of sand
falling, falling through fingers,
dry ruffling of feathers.

But the earth turns,
air begins to dart and puff,
spring corn flattens; cell by cell,
gravity bent, blades are sucked
into movement; trees sway, leaning,
longing for the threatening storm.

# Give Me the Eyes of a Stranger

Give me the eyes of a stranger
to see Maam and Leenane anew,
bog, bracken, lake, exaggerated hills,
land layered in mist,
blue and yellow, grey and green,
the colours that Paul Henry stole.

Give me the eyes of a stranger
to see through a gap in the clouds
that mythical space where
our narrative was hatched,
the triple trace of islands
swallowing Atlantic ire,
spitting rain across the bay
with its cargo of regret,
the beckoning dead.

Give me the eyes of a stranger
to understand stories
better than statistics,
the mysteries of savagery,
grandiosity, improbable visions,
heritage illegibly written
by some untraceable race;
to find our whereabouts is nowhere
with a smile on its face;
to wear rootlessness with panache,
no plans beyond tomorrow's
definite uncertainty.

Give me the eyes of a stranger
to drink of the liquid dark
and then, well liquored,
feel an inexplicable love,
subservient to no rule
other than the astonishment of
death gone to seed and sprouting.

Give me the eyes of a stranger
to see danger petering out,
washed safe in a lake;
Connemara winds re-settled,
dancing on ribbons of road
around the flanks of the Pins.

## Milestone

A wish
to draw a line at seventy
forgive everything
forget nothing
cross the line
peel off the false moustache
find a cave in the hills
paint my ache upon the walls
and leave it there –
a new order
approaching silence.

## Trstenik, Croatia

Trstenik is empty,
a blank page, awaiting record:
off-the-beaten-track history
of fragmented half-forgotten
harbour hamlets twisting in the sun.

There is no coffee; the Mljet ferry has left;
a child's swing screeches complaint;
roped boats nod assent to their reflections;
crabs scrawl memos on washed rock;
butterflies, boulevardiers in flashy suits,
discrediting mortality.

Nothing to do but borrow time
in a taverna, dilute it with Dingac
and watch beautiful, botched buildings
climb a slope over craggy boulders
towards the vineyards
terracing across the mountain.

Wine in a glass, wine in the fields,
the whole day drunk and barely standing.

# The Work

*for Kerry Hardie*

All day reclaiming the winter stream,
mud as dark as the spent black wood
which fouled its path. The stench
leaving an imprint beneath my skin.

Always this need to bring water
to its clearing, to free some withheld thing;
echoes of my mother and father enmeshed
in the root tangle of cress and waterweed.

Because patterns repeat themselves and I keep
thinking of you Kerry, over and again
attending to the metal of your being, polishing
its essence; turning yourself to find again

fingerprints to clear away. Evening
settling its blue mist on the November field
led me to leave down mud and boots and tools
at the door of the yellow-lit house, knowing

there will always be this work. Be trapped things.
Always that which flows seeking containment,
boundaries, ensnaring itself in the flounder
of longing and mistake making.

And it is the nature of elements that shine
to also tarnish, in the same way
that the expansive moon, which once more
silvers running water, will in time diminish;

yet I also know, you will leave here brighter than you came.

# Pioneer

The last memories of her husband have been sewn
into a quilt which barely warms her nights.
After bad dreams, their son and daughter sleep
furled beneath small flags of nightshirt
and brushed cotton sleeve worn thin.
Four summers and their harsh winters
have passed since she marked his grave.
Her own parents write, begging her home,
begging, before the children run quite wild.
Formally, they offer a second cousin
with land near York, ask she seriously consider
this most suitable widower of some renown.
Their letters go unanswered.

She is loosely moored between two worlds,
anchored only by the children,
for all they have ever drunk is from the well of this place.
And what flows in her now
is rainwater, woodsmoke, silence reflected
on the lake surface; leaves turned,
hair snagged on briars. Stones. The small,
white feathers that line nests.
She is sung with fox bark and pheasant call.
Creatures roost in her thoughts, her days
are measured by the slink, the leap, the pounce,
the pitched balance of wings breaking into flight.
She too moves in feral ways.

And lavender soap on Sundays is a fine gauze veil,
though the men in church stare with downcast eyes,
she knows what it is they smell on her, and, wary of hunters,

is afraid. She lives where the long road from town
meets the trackless purple mountains. Some nights
leaning into the silver shadows at her door
she wonders who will come for her first,
for the quiet is also pregnant with alcohol and laughter,
with a swagger some miles off, and there are eyes
that watch from the mauve shadow inland;
if she stood still long enough,
had she interest in belonging,
they would take her as one of their own tribe.

All she has carved for herself is a small square of land,
free of chickweed and scutch-grass, soil abundant with seed.

# JARLATH FAHY

## the day I fell in love with a housecoat in otooles supervalu tuam the haberdashery section

i couldn't believe my eyes
there between the mops
and the buckets the coal
scuttles and the delph
with the wee small cottages on them
besides the sets of black cats
you know the ones one cat
standing two cats sitting
all joined together by a chain
around their necks
there it was a small rail
of housecoats my god
just like my grandmother wore
you could have knocked me over
with a feather duster
the air was suffused with lavender
you know the polish they used to
use for polishing floors
i couldn't help myself
i couldn't take my eyes off it
i had to put it on the cut of it
small red flowers the navy colour
overwhelming the feeling unbelievable
the store detective didn't seem
to think so *what are you doing*
he asked me *are you some kind*
*of transvestite or something*
*what are you at* – *no* i says *it's*

*the housecoat my grandmother*
*used to wear try one on it feels*
*bloody marvellous  are you serious*
he says *jeeze it is my granny wore*
*one of them too* and he tried one on
then the manager arrived *what the*
*hell is going on here* he says
and we convinced him to try one on too
and before we knew where we were
weren't we singing *there were three lovely*
*lassies from bannion* and dancing down the aisles

## Absence

I enter the woods
haunted by the absence
of your presence.

Sunlight filters
on summer leaves
falling to earth.
I caress a leaf
on my doubting palm,
retrace a final journey.

The life this form embodied
has not departed.
The breath of life
that cradled this leaf
on its descent embraced
your soul on its ascent.

I leave these woods
lightened by the Presence
in your absence.

# Pride

My brother, David, was quieter than usual; my mother was louder than ever. Anne Doyle read the news on the radio and my mother kept shouting at the tuning dial that Mayo was going to win.

David was driving her Toyota. She sat in the front seat, waving miniature flags at strangers and accosting motorists at traffic lights, her head stuck out the window like a dog in summer. They looked away embarrassed or stared ahead with blank faces. My brother shot her a glance of sympathy that seemed to question her sanity. It was the way he arched his eyebrows. With her beaming smile, she glossed over his disapproval.

'Aren't you excited, son?' she asked.

'I'm driving, Mam,' he said, changing gear.

'And he's mortified, Mam' I said, 'will you calm down.'

'Calm' she roared, 'Calm? Isn't there time enough to be calm when I'm long gone and Mayo is not about to bring home Sam. This is a day to feel alive, a day for greatness.'

'I've a headache,' David said, as we inched along the North Quays, sandwiched between taxis. He spoke almost in a whisper. My mother pretended not to hear him. I ignored him too, and started to daydream about the girl I used to be.

'Look, a 32A, on its way to Ballymun, that's the bus I used to call the 'unmarried mothers convention,"' I said.

'Lovely,' said my mother, not listening. I saw myself, at nineteen, head resting on the cold windowpane. I remember the smells: damp rain jackets, marijuana and vinegar-drenched chips. The passengers seemed a different species to me. Track-suited boyfriends with pin-prick pupils told teenage mums to shut their gobs; volatile voices on the checkered green seats. And I sat quietly taking these other lives in, wondering how it felt to mainline in the morning, what life was like for those with nothing but toxic brown powder to aspire to, what it meant to be one of the people in the tower blocks who lived walking distance from me and my life in Dublin City University.

Drumcondra had been many things to me. We drove by the yellow door behind which I first felt love, in the single bed by the whistling window, where socks were never removed, when day and night was tangled up. He showed his love for me with wheatabix and hot milk, the top layer of skin carefully scooped off because I hated the slimy texture. His poem said I had blatant beauty and that I brought trouble on myself.

I shifted in the back seat, breathing out regret. It seized me again like it always did, every time I passed the net curtained corporation houses on Dorset Street. I will never know which house it was, but I know my wrists were once held so tight the red marks would not fade. I kissed those boys that night because they wanted to kiss me, and because I didn't know who I was kissing. I realize now that as I sauntered home drunk and bumped into the wrong people it could have been a lot worse, and wasn't. I went to College expecting something other than what I found there. Time had now passed, times had now changed. Everything was to teach us something, I thought, before telling David to indicate at the next junction.

The streets screamed colour. Bunting in tomato red and school-uniform green framed pub windows. A group of lads brushed against the bonnet, flags draped over shoulders, friends unified in anticipation; fresh from the cheap hotels in run-down Georgian houses on Parnell Square. Crossmolina had come to O'Connell Street. Ticket-less, we traveled on. It was enough to be within earshot of the stadium.

'Park here,' I told my brother, 'I lived in that house once.'

Back then I used to curse the GAA for impinging on my final-year thesis as I flicked redundant earplugs from my desk. The atmosphere would seep into the redbrick cottage and into my garret room. I smoked my Marlboro reds, tipping ash onto the unsuspecting heads of fans as they marched towards destiny. I would see them laugh and drink and stumble, and I would wallow in the sorrow of my situation, wishing my unwritten words would flow so that I could graduate into a world without footnotes.

'Come on, Son' said my mother, slapping David's back. He almost tripped as we made our way to the pub. Laughter was everywhere, the hearty, cackling, giddy kind; exaggerated nervous laughter that followed the beat of the Gardai who ambled through the throngs on time and a half. People wanted to know the best route, the short cut, the quickest way, but all roads led to Croke Park, a place of communal pride, where lost dreams could be resurrected.

It was a day with a license for the good life. Like Christmas, normal rules didn't apply. My mother was chattering, enjoying her status as a Westport woman, less mother and more herself. Petrified of growing old, she chased atmosphere in her time off. The more people, the better; sardines in tins and she was happy. Nursing drug addicts at night, she knew all about the grief of others. But it never prepared her for loss. She listened to the stories of the living dead. 'Addicts are the most complex of people', she says, 'they hang on to hurt and their greatest fear is what they'll never be.' Mam enjoyed the night shift. She liked company, especially these people, because they made her feel fortunate. Whenever a new batch came in, she would look up their charts and scan the dates of birth for years she recognized. She would then measure the mess of their lives against her children's success.

A group of teenagers skipped past, blowing whistles. 'The atmosphere, you can't beat the atmosphere,' Mam repeated, craning her neck, surveying the crowds as if they had all turned up just for her.

First cousins with whom we shared our childhood joined us. They were the real deal. Both parents came from the County Mayo. We were the half casts, especially today.

'Where are the Lily Whites? Didn't I tell you all along they were the Lily Shites,' said Sean. 'Time to shift your loyalty, was it, I suppose needs must,' he sniggered. He was three months older than me to the day. As toddlers, they made us sit on potties and pose for photographs.

Big screen televisions hung high on the walls. I looked around. Smiling eyes, nodding grins, full pints: we were all friends here.

'Well, will we do it, do ye think, t'is our chance, t'is deserved?' said an older man, who was sitting on a high stool wearing his funeral suit. He was alone amongst his own. Armed with his chat up line, he addressed every punter who approached the counter. He kept winking in our direction, like a toy doll with a fault.

'David, look at rip van winkle over there,' I said. My brother, who normally welcomed such characters for their innate ability to make us laugh, didn't respond. I suspected he was in a mood. He could be quiet in a way that I resented, impenetrable, a vault. I wanted everyone to know how it felt to be me. I wondered what was wrong with him. Why was he sulking?

Outside, the pavement lined with silver kegs became home, the hearth, where punters swapped stories to pass the time until the time, when the whistle would blow and the real story began to unfold. David was drinking Cidona from a bottle with a straw. Leaning against the whitewashed wall, I watched him hunker down to a child's line of vision. He tilted his head to the side and rested it on the palm of his right hand. He looked like a refugee in a land of sameness.

There was standing room only as the game kicked off. We stood in the front bar, close to the doors. The draft was welcome. David stood beside me looking older than his eighteen years.

'Are you alright?' I asked.

'No, I still have that headache. I think I'm going to go,' he said ironing his brow with the back of his hand.

'Already,' I said, before a surge of movement made me spill my drink.

Suddenly every second person was a jack-in-the-box.

'Go onnnnn,' the crowds roared, as stockpiled spittle sprinkled out from their mouths. Fists flew into the air. The smoky pub became the stock exchange floor. Random shrieks reverberated. It was a chorus of the affirmative, the negative, the yes, the no, the obligatory cursing and the sharp intakes of breath. One woman looked like a child trying to inflate a balloon, both cheeks pumped up as she sat exhaling through pursed lips. Her husband had one word on repeat, 'Jesus.'

'Tell Mam,' David said before slipping away, fading out, leaving the mayhem behind. I, wanting to stay, watched him go, assuming that he must have got some bad news from the skinny blonde he was dating, the ballet dancer with the piercing green eyes. He was always so full of pride, never able to show a weakness. He did look gaunt, his shoulders hunched, but it had to be more than just a headache. 'Take care,' I said.

Mayo was leading, just about. Half time was a chance to celebrate. It might be the only one and so people clinked glasses, crossed fingers and sang out of tune ballads.

'Where's David?' my mother asked, as she reappeared from her ring-side seat.

'He wasn't feeling very well and went home,' I told her. Perplexed, she wanted details.

'What do you mean, he went home? Why – was he sick? What did he say, where is he?' Answers were not necessary. She borrowed my phone to call him before the game resumed, a race of questions sprinting down the line.

'David, love,' she shouted, 'Are you alright, why did you go, are you sick, where are you now? Are you okay to drive, why did you not say something?' He assured her that he could drive and was going home to Kildare to bed. That conversation was enough for her to switch back. She was now more of a mother and less of herself.

Those with seats secured them. Territorial emotions ran high. That was mine. There's someone sitting there. You're in my place. People bruised past us, anxious to get a good vantage point for the second crucial half of the match. The next hour was the culmination of dedication, for the team and the supporters, who had invested so many rainy weekends waiting for this. The colds caught and the tears shed had been worth it for the fervent belief in every pair of eyes watching the screen that day that they could be something better.

Mayo lost by five points. A last-minute goal for the other side and the alcohol turned sour. We spilled out onto the streets, feeling cheated. Discarded streamers lay strewn amongst the plastic pint glasses. The sun had disappeared, behind the Dublin Mountains, but it was too soon to go home. We went to a Chinese restaurant. I left to use the bathroom and my phone rang, echoing in the mirrored room.

'Is Mam with you?' David said, before dropping the phone.

I could hear it hop off the kitchen floor.

'Sorry,' he said. I crossed my legs.

'I'll get her to call you in a minute, what's the matter, are you still feeling sick?' I could envision him nod as I pushed the toilet door open.

The food had arrived. My mother was rolling her pancake into a cylinder; thinly sliced cucumber strips peeked out the top. A blob of plum sauce fell from the end, landing on the white tablecloth.

'David called,' I told her. The pancake fell apart.

'What did he say; is he alright? How did he sound – I better ring him,' she said with her mouth full of food. She called her son, and dessert was cancelled.

Hours later, in a few lines of dialogue with the doctor, the improbable became the probable. In a family room at the Mater Hospital, things that happened only to other people had suddenly happened to us. David got meningitis on the day Mayo lost the all Ireland final again. The fluorescent light overhead flickered and I remember hearing a drunken voice from the street outside shouting, 'We were robbed.'

# Heaven

and he used to repeat words and phrases like an invocation, or an incantation, and I remember my feet dangling over the front of the cart, and it had no sides, and if I fell forward I was gone body and soul into the gravel passing underneath in a blur, and he stood above me connected to the horse by the reins and his voice, and when the horse lifted his tail I had to lean away, but I didn't blame the horse because it was blinkered, and even if he could see behind it wasn't his fault the flies like the sun, and mammy wasn't there with soft words and her scarf the same colour as the sea beyond the hill on a day like this,

and Father Lynskey had bad skin, like Heaney's field in winter, reciting the parishioners names, one shilling, one shilling, and they don't have two pennies to rub together, six pence, God help us, two and six, two and six, Master Brearty five shillings, Doctor Cassidy ten shillings, Mister Ryan ten shillings, and mammy's sister, aunt Kate, said "It's time they cut that out," and I wished he hadn't bent down so close to me oozing of stale tobacco, and he said, "She's in heaven Martin", and missus Heaney, who never smiled and always kept hens, said, "She's in a better place," to daddy who found it hard to look at anybody, especially Pa Heaney who fenced off land that didn't belong to him,

and I was thinking about heaven beside daddy's boots clacking on the stones, and grand aunt Delia held my hand and had to let it go for a second to blow her nose, twice, the second time very loud and even daddy looked over, and she was talking to aunt Kate, who was a nurse in the north of England, and she said, "Mary never ate butter", and grand aunt Delia said, "Is that right", "And that was why she wasted away so quickly", "She wasted away to nothing", and I was thinking about that while they were talking, how could she say she wasted away to nothing when her face was still there, and her eyes closed, and her fingers clasping her wooden beads, and she could be asleep, and I could go back to bed and pretend with my eyes closed and wait for her voice,

and daddy rocked over and back, over and back, "as it was in the beginning", and mammy's brother, uncle Jamie, who had travelled all around the world when he was younger, was standing there, and his fingers were long like mammy's, and when his eye caught mine he nodded down at me slowly, and I looked away, and Father Lynskey wheezed when he started the Hail Mary, before

people were finished, as if he was duty bound to keep their beads moving without a break, "is now and ever shall be", and two of daddy's brothers had shovels, and when the earth made a hollow sound daddy looked away towards the sea, and the sky had cotton wool clouds, and grand aunt Delia coughed, and when she coughed again uncle Jamie took her arm, and a big black crow watched from the branch that grew through the gable of the old ruin,

and I could smell stale onions over the smoke and beer dregs in Ryans when grand aunt Delia leaned into my face and said, "Why don't you play with your cousins", we never visited them, they never visited us, the O'Tooles from the far side of the mountain, pulling and dragging out of each other, and when they saw me at the church porch they just looked at me with their mouths open, and I said nothing, and they said nothing, and I said, "Daddy where's heaven", holding on to the pocket of his coat, and it was lumpy where the seams come together, and he said, "Why don't you play with your cousins", and I couldn't say that I didn't want to, and aunt Joan with blonde hair, who worked in the same hospital as aunt Kate, put a glass of fizzy orange in front of me and she didn't ask me if I wanted a straw, she just smiled at me, and I made the orange last when my father went to the bar, and aunt Dorothy looked at me and said, "Isn't he getting big", and someone else said, "He's a fine man", and I was rocking forward and back avoiding their eyes looking down on me,

and grand aunt Delia had a box of plates and saucers with a faded blue line around the edge that she said she painted on herself, years ago, and Father Lynskey was first at the table, and I noticed his fingers were brown, "Have you anything stronger", he said to aunt Dorothy, and he spent most of the time talking to aunt Joan, and he said, "It's terrible taking all your cigarettes like that", because he left his in another jacket, and missus Heaney brought a big lump of boiled bacon, and grand aunt Delia said "You can never judge a book by its cover," and aunt Joan overheard her and laughed, and grand aunt Delia coughed, and aunt Kate said, "You better get that seen to or you'll be next," and uncle Jamie went missing and aunt Dorothy said, "He promised," and I could see him through the net curtains with doves in flight leaning against a post and his body shaking,

and when the house was on fire from the setting sun I asked daddy "Where's heaven," and he took in a deep sigh and I asked again "Where's heaven," and he had no answer, and if he did he didn't tell me, and I followed his boots up to the top of

the hill and he didn't need to look behind to know I was following him, and there was a swell making diamonds that turned white where mammy said the souls of sailors were lost, but I think she only said that to frighten me off the sea, and I remembered a basket and a blanket flattening the grass and we were waiting for his shirt and his smile, and she said he was turning hay to let the wind and the sun at it, like the turf, the smell of the turf got into everything, mammy said, even her best dress, and a grey gull whistled after its mother, and the sea was orange over the sand, and the seaweed was rising and falling, and the mauve mountains kissed the clouds, and I was looking at all the things she had shown me, and daddy stood looking, and I was hoping he'd say something and it didn't matter what it would be, anything, there's a lot of dandelions this year, that's a big swell, there's weather coming, anything,

and going through the gate, I walked in the dry ruts, and he never said "Be careful," or "Mind the thorn," the thorn with white flowers in May that mammy said were beautiful, and we were standing on a rock that came up out of the earth in a gentle curve, a rock with white lines, and he said they were marble and mammy said they were not marble, "Those lines came up out of the bowels of the earth, how could you have marble in granite," and he stood corrected, and I was wondering how the great explosion of fire could look so peaceful, and moss creeping up on it, like a whale somebody thought was an island, mammy told me that story going to bed and she said she didn't know if it was true or not,

and I could smell the salt, and the swallows were saying good night, and the waves were shaping the sand, and all daddy said was, "Don't ever forget," and I was trying to understand what he meant when he said it again, "Don't ever forget," and he said it with conviction as if forgetting would be the end of everything, and he didn't say what it was I should never forget, something that had no name, like the wind that drifted a feathery seed past my face, or a gannet roosting on the stone wall that criss crossed the hill, or a ram mammy reversed out the back door to keep good luck in the house, or the slow teapot she loved because the spout reminded her of a swan,

and missus Heaney was closing the gate at the bottom of the avenue, it wasn't really an avenue with trees and wooden fencing, we called it the avenue because our house was so far back from the road and everything had to be carted in by hand, and at the back door there was a basket with a cloth very neatly tucked in,

and under the cloth were white eggs, white like the marble in the granite, and daddy just nodded his head as if he was agreeing with some thought he had, but he didn't tell me what it was,

and we were cracking our eggs when the door opened, and Father Lynskey was standing there, "Its very dark in here," and my father offered him a seat and an egg, and I sat well back, and he didn't want a seat or an egg, he had plenty of eggs at home, Peggie doesn't know what to do with all the eggs he has, and he looked into the empty hearth and he asked, "Will the young lad be starting school, he must be old enough now," was he only making conversation, and I thought of Miss Kane and her hair severely hidden under a scarf in the pew ahead of us, and she was a hundred times more serious than missus Heaney, and I could feel my stomach beginning to collapse, and Father Lynskey didn't get to say whatever it was he wanted to say because I must have turned white and started breathing as if someone was after me, and then I could smell his tobacco examining what kind of stuff I was made of, telling me there was no need to be that afraid of him, he was only God's servant on this earth and he'd call back another time and keep an eye on him,

and daddy lifted the window and the cool night came in with the sound of the sea, and I was still feeling pale, and I couldn't look at an egg, and daddy held my two small hands in his and we rocked over and back, over and back, and the shadow of a large moth danced on the ceiling over the yellow lamp, and I closed my eyes, and I could hear his voice rising above the waves, in a slow air, and I didn't know if they were words, or if he was lilting, and I was thinking about the white places on the sea, and the lines on the smooth stone, and the flowers on the thorn, and I don't know how long we stayed like that

# Are you ready?

When the row with the wife has gone
on for over a week and your neck
and lower back hurt from sleeping
on the dirty green sofa –
and when the chips you got in McDonalds
Drive-Thru fall in to the space
around the handbrake and you're sorry
now that your toe-nail clippings
are still there, and you made the mistake
of putting  your only white shirt
into the washing machine
along with the lawnmower,
are you ready?

Are you ready to admit that it was you
who ran over Bozo in 1997 and broke
his front legs, that the hundred pounds
she saved for Santa went on the fourth
placed certainty in the three ten at Newmarket,
that it was you who ran up the phone bill
on the sex lines,
that you do sometimes drink and drive,
that you occasionally wear
your wife's lingerie,
that the job interview really was golf,
that you do secretly fancy Susan Kelly,
that you once voted for the PDs?

Are you ready?
Are you ready to admit?
Are you ready to admit
that maybe it was you that was in the wrong
all along?

# A Beautiful Day

It was madness, sheer madness. Any sane person would have been out of there, downing a pint in some nearby pub or tucked up at home in front of a good soccer match. But here we were at the old power station across the border, arse-deep in a river, the rain lashing down on us. Fishing. I had never done it before. The cast and spin, the trail and flick. I hadn't a clue. And the patience it took. Nothing was happening. Nothing. Everything around me seemed to have a negative mindset. The river, the rain, the wind in the drenched trees, the fish, if there were any. Part of me knew that if I could see myself from the road, I would be thinking, 'What a nutter!' I'd always thought that about men I saw fishing, especially ones arse-deep in the middle of a river in the lashing rain.

Another part of me was beginning to get into it. The rain ran off my bulging cape, the waders kept me dry. I still had my problems with the casting, but slowly I was acquiring a kind of technique. My younger brother Jim was the expert; Danny was his side-kick. Jim showed me five minutes of the basics, then said he'd leave me to get the hang of it. He kept an eye on me, shouting bits of advice across at me. Most of what he shouted got carried away with the rain. But being with the two of them began to feel good. Each one of us covered our own stretch of the river, still somehow connected like a set of navigation points.

When I got a bite, Jim rushed over. 'Hold tight. Bring her in nice and easy now.' He stayed with me until I had it in the net, then waded out into the river again. Getting the barb out wasn't as bad as I thought it would be. I tried to twist it out humanely at first. But no way. Then I ripped it out. I didn't look at what I was doing. Just did it. The fish still jiggled a bit until I used the stone.

But Danny's salmon was the real thing; landing her lasted about half an hour.

'Don't let her break away!' Jim screamed. 'She'll snap the line. Hold on to her.' He kept his eyes on the way the fish was manoeuvring, the way she played the line. 'Let her have plenty of slack, Danny. Jesus, she's a big one. Let her run with it.'

Jim was beating through the water; Danny did his best to do what he was told. They'd been friends for years, fixed up cars together. And women. That's why they understood each other better than Jim and I ever would

'I think she got away, Jim. She's not pulling any more.'

'She's a clever one, Danny. She's still there alright. Hold on to her. She'll be back in a minute. There she goes!'

I could hear the jerk that went through Danny's rod, thought it would snap in two as a bright flash shot out over the grey of the river. Something inside me wanted the line to break.

This fish deserved to live. But no way was I going to say that.

'Tire her out, Danny! She's giving you a run for your money.'

The tail of the fish was kicking in the water as she hit out at whatever was holding her back. I could feel the energy in her, defiance in the way she struggled.

'Okay, Danny. Wind her in. Nice and slow now.' The fish bolted at the first tug of the line and shot off. The reel whirred loudly as the fish drew the line with it into deeper water. Then something jammed.

'Fuck it, Jim!'

'Hold on, Danny!'

Danny's rod looked as if it wouldn't hold out much longer. Jim waded through the water and belted the locked reel with the side of his fist. It must have hurt, but the line was freed.

'Wind her in again now, Danny. She must be nearly beat.'

This time my younger brother was wrong. As if she had heard him, as if the only thing she wanted now was to prove how wrong he was, the fish took off again. Danny was splashing after her, trying to keep up.

'She's a good one.' Jim rushed behind him, laughing. 'She had us good'n fooled that time.'

She didn't want to be caught. Every fibre inside her was

primed against it. But each time she pulled on the line, the barb lodged itself deeper in the roof of her mouth. That was how it worked. Even I understood that now. If she hadn't managed to snap the line when her energy was at its peak, now that she was tiring, her chances of getting away were gone. All Danny had to do was let her flag herself out and then wind her in. Eventually he got her into shallow water again and Jim heaved her out.

Her tail still flapped. She was a magnificent creature, dappled and shimmering with lost life.

'Jesus, there's some weight in her. I can hardly hold her. You got yourself a whopper of a one there, Danny.'

Jim cradled the salmon in his arms while Danny worked at the barb. There was no way it would come out easily. She flailed and twitched as Danny's hands worked at her mouth.

'Fuck this, Jim,' Danny said.

'Give it a good hard jerk,' Jim told him.

The shock kicked through the fish's body, then it lay motionless.

'Some prize for a day's fishing.' Jim held out his arms full of fish. 'You're a lucky fucker, Danny Gilmore.'


A year later Danny was shot in the back by the Paratroopers. He was running away from them. Everybody was running away, trying to get behind something solid. The bullet went in one side and out the other. Danny gasped and toppled forward. A priest, waving a white handkerchief, crawled over to him to give him the last rites.

After Danny's burial, they would find his mother in the middle of the night with a blanket over his grave, trying to keep the cold off him.

## Study of Lug

He was born with a hole in his head
but so were the majority of his generation.
This gave way to that veneration
of dead heroes, and civil service.

Yet I cannot think of him without smiling.
Standing powerless, his arms flung apart.
He was acquainted with small birds,
and smart in soft slippers.

One hand was a nest, the other a hard acorn.
But he was not comic, with a view of
a dunghill, a rat-hole, a dog, an ass, a pig.

I held his dry fingers like a dowser's twig.
Shook a bit when I found no human thing.
His soul accomplished immobility, having
been without hope too long, his feet bled
when he tore them from the clay, and
overnight his hair turned grey.

# KEVIN O'SHEA

## New Trick For Jessie

The vet looks more like a
professor of lost languages,
perpetually sad at their passing,
than a handler of departing animals.

Then, with the practiced flourish
of a vaudeville mesmerist,
The Great Rudolfo reveals
his syringe full of neon-pink
like a new blend of Fairy liquid.

We watch closely
as he searches her paws
for just the right vein
and spot his secret move
that rams the plunger home.

Falling for his patter
*She didn't feel a thing*
we gasp
at the dénouement
as he touches the surface
of a still vivid eyeball
without a blink.

When my mind takes
the closing step
I hope to find a magician
to conjure a final illusion.

I, too, want to be tricked.

# LORNA SHAUGHNESSY

## Carran

I could not say
I felt like a walking miracle
as we travelled south
on the first day of spring.

Snow on the Burren
fleshed out skeletal stones,
stopped gaps in the walls
so the air could not pass
and the valley sank deeper
into smothered soundlessness.

Three swans heaved across the lake
in burdensome flight,
the huff and cronk of the long pull
echoless on the blanketed stone.

I went to the well
in search of no more miracles
than those already worked:
the vanishing act conjured
by the surgeon's hand,
the venomous magic
that coils around the cup.

I went to leave flowers,
draw water and listen to its song,
gather round the fire
to hear words recited,
familiar lines sung
and recall absent voices.

To be thankful
at the end of a long year
of days when I hated
having to be grateful.

On that two-faced morning
I could look back
at my bloodied footprints
and see them fill with snow,
then turn to face the blank page.

# LORNA SHAUGHNESSY

## Vantage Point

Strange how new rites spring from the old,
without these liturgies of our own making
we can no longer conceive the day.
So we stop, again, at this vantage point,
and looking out over the lake in its limestone bowl,
take a step back from the year, and breathe.

Too cold to go al fresco, we huddle in the car,
cherish the heat of flask tea balanced on our laps,
begin a new year's weave of stories, starting at the centre,
one folding over another like the rushes of a cross;
the oldest need, the need for green at winter's end.

Stories pass hand over hand with cups and shared bread,
braiding years, miles, selves, until the wax lost
in the forging of a cross by the silversmith of Agadez
solidifies today in votive candles lit by the well.

Your poem in my mouth is unsummoned communion,
the moment's grace a pilgrimage to ourselves.
The breast-bone cracks open, the heart whelms,
swollen as this lake with winter rain.

## Death and the Post Office

The job they're given is fairly simple.
Find the place,
go in for half an hour and discuss the settlement.
Consider, if it's appropriate,
the few antiques: the safe,
the signs, the switchboard.
Glance at the books, the electrics.
Perhaps fill out some forms.
But these aul' ones, these Cathleens, these Annies,
they can be fierce long-winded.
For some of our lads their ways
are just too compelling.

Some accept a drink, some'll have lunch.
We'd a Polish guy who took
a ninety-two-year-old out in the van.
She showed him a ball alley.
Fair enough: dozens of ghosts
and no graffiti. But if you're not direct
about the job? You understand,
we've had to weed out the dreamers.
Immunity to stories, I find,
is the primary quality.
You don't want to be sitting at an old table,
under a clock that strikes you

as fabulously loud.
Or find yourself cradled by the past,
thinking a man need venture
no further west than the brink he meets
in a mouthful of milky tea.
If the archive-harbouring frailty

of the postmistress soothes you;
if her wit grants you the lost farm
and maternity of the world;
if her isolated, dwindling village, a place
without a pub or a shop,
whose nearest decent

sized town is itself desperately quiet –
if these things move you …
What I mean is, if you can't meet
a forgotten countryside
head on, and calmly dismantle her,
fold her up, carry her out,
and ship her back
to Head Office, however ambiguous,
however heavy-handed or fateful,
however bloody poignant
the whole affair might seem to you;
if you can't stand your ground

when a steep moment
of hospitable chat and reminiscence
might tempt you to put
your mobile phone on silent,
or worse, blinded by plates of fruit cake,
to switch it off completely;
if you cannot accompany
an inevitable change, knowing
you did not cause these people, these ways, to vanish,
and if you will not sign off
on expired things for us,
then, I'm sorry, but you are not our man.

# Independence

His mother and his sisters gave up on him
in his forties. There were admirers in the town,
opportunities in Galway and Dublin.
Yet doggedly he built his vintage solitude.

And even in the years when the odd echo
of his origins could reach him still, in the dawn
of his middle-age loneliness, he persevered.
Suicide spoke, but he'd the same deafness ready.

Lately though, at night, his blood gathers itself
against that will. It ladles across his mind
an early vanity: memories of being wanted,
memories, some fictive, of being silver-tongued.
While his heart, a kind of fox, climbs down to the lake
and begs the dark to strike or bless the cottage.

# In Other Words

I'd like to gloss your post-modern grin
with a labio-dental fricative to begin.
Then, a bilabial plosive.

God knows what would come out, if I started to use
my west-of-the-Shannon round vowels,
which you are colonizing.

As you purse your lips to front yours,
I notice that it goes very well with your chic-about-town suit.
You speak foreign D4 to the men in my parts,
who respect sibilants that don't make a difference.
Know that SHTOP is surprise, not a rural marker
separating them from the wise fellas
up at the University.
Or a noun,
something they would do to sort out
A poseur like you.

You flex your intellectual biceps
obsessed, not only by your manhood
but by the kind of man you are.
The genre, an obtrusive voice,
your life, a metafiction,
a revised identity.

Now, your grandmother, a professional woman
who walked to school from May to October
in her bare feet
is unsure about her story.
It is not one of the images you are staying with today.
Your voice echoes in the 1970s box architecture

of the new Irish University,
hollow as Plato's Cave.
The sign of the times no more than
the minute's silence for Guinness,
for Irish before the singing of the national anthem.

The men in my parts still check the sky for the weather,
are ensconced in a world that loves them,
will turn up at the funeral,
pay respects to one of the best.
You wish your words still had meaning like theirs.
It's what you left behind,
men pulling their wellies up over wool socks to go out on the land,
while you lace up your expensive trainers
to jog on an asphalt running track.

You can hear the chortling of a bird
coaxing you back to your senses.
It would be too much like innocence
To know whether it is a lark in the morning,
a sparrow chattering, or a robin claiming territory.
You put up the volume, adjust your earphones,
check the zapper for the electric gate is in your pocket,
home is only a block away.

# Demeter Does Not Remember

Persephone, her shadowed daughter
in the portico, peeping through the cracked wall.
Or what she said to keep her away.

Or what she gave her to dam her legs
when blood flowed,
red into the underworld.

Demeter cannot remember her first smile or teeth,
the words she made.
Persephone would have liked to know.

Now, a woman, she looks into the still lake of her dreams,
filled by the torrents of the Styx.
What does she see?

She walks away heartbroken
from the quivering reflection.
Cries out, 'Demeter is not me.'

## Larry and Barry

A Galway and a Suffolk ram;
employed on our farm
to fuck.

When the midwife is due
Larry and Barry are left to themselves
and two into Alpha doesn't go.

Over the years
every business blow
reduced blood
from torrent to trickle.

When Larry developed meningitis
he was taken into care.
Barry had a look
that struck me dumb.

I will never be able to tell Barry
I was there
when life left his body.

A mountain crumbling into nothing.

# An Unknown Blue

I want to be still
as a folded note
   left on a table
before sunrise,

silent as the crease
concealing words
   that will not
have been read –

for all intents unopened;
just a strand
   shimmering
on the dark edge of a knife.

NICKI GRIFFIN

# Shoreditch

Sirens.
A single star.

Clouds fast forward
spiked
with leaning cranes.

Above the sallow
hunkering sky,
glutted with city lights,
gibbets leer.

Bonuses hang
from scaffold hooks,
taunt the tent-livers
of St Paul's
with Square Mile money.

In the park a man lays out
his plastic-bag life,
overlooked
by city workers
in bright-lit boxes.

# The Horologist's Dream of Silence

A watch stripped of all embellishments
and the vanities of his craft. A masterwork.
Last night he dreamt of it again. In the strange

half-light of his workshop time breaths
in his hands. He leans down to it slowly
as though listening for the heartbeat of a child.

He hears an orchestra of whispers there: the spinning
wheel and spindle, the move and counter move
of the ratchet, the centrifuge of the hammer.

It is time made audible as music or a sound so pure
it is the closest he has come to silence. He listens.
All the lost voices of his childhood return

from the darkness, the crack of gunshot in the streets
at daybreak, the heavy boots climbing the staircase.
If he could only tell them he survived he might

redeem their sacrifice, make time whole again.
He rubs the sleep from his eyes – will go on trying.

# Dead People

Darren says his weird uncle has some pictures in his garage. Pictures of dead people, he says, and he looks at me. I am smoking my last cigarette, feeling the smoke curve around my teeth.

'You want to see dead people?' Darren says.

I push my hair out of my face so I can look at Darren. He's wearing his birthday jacket. It's black with an ice-sheen. He wants me to give him a present too. Something good, he says. Something he can think about before he goes to sleep. Darren thinks he's romantic. He thinks I'm his. He says he likes my mystery face. He tells my friends I'm the kind you wait for. I know he's lying. My best friend Freda said Darren waits for no one. He didn't wait for her – but maybe you're different, Freda said.

Darren says he likes me because I've got ideas and I read books. One day he showed off how nice he was to me by asking me to read from the book in my bag.

'Who the fuck is Emily? said Darren's friend Josie.

She chewed her gum and fingered pages in the book.

'A writer,' I said.

'See?' Darren said. 'Read a bit,' he said to me.

So I read it. I can't remember whereabouts it was in the book I read, but it was good. I like all those words that say things. I like the way a sentence shows up like a picture in my head. Mum says I've got one of those minds you've got to be careful about. I want too much weird stuff after reading books. Her sister was the same and she ended up dead somewhere. Mum's warned me that if I do anything with Darren – you wash yourself out, you hear me?

Darren tries to touch me too much. He comes round to play cards with my step-dad, Kevin. Kevin says I couldn't do any better. Kevin says my books breed spiders in the house. Once

Kevin hit me straight across my face and Mum just got quiet in the kitchen. She smoked the whole afternoon with the telly on. Kevin said I was the sort of girl you had to keep your eyes on.

Once I let Darren do something. He said it would be nice. It felt like a warm slug in my mouth, and I threw up afterwards. Darren took a photo on his phone of my face. He said even with puke on my chin, I looked like one of the girls in the old paintings he's seen in his uncle's garage. Flat face girls with creamy skin and gold bands in their hair.

Freda says I look ugly sometimes. She says I don't know what girls are supposed to do for boys. You don't just kiss it or lick it. You do other things as well. Things like Mum does in bed with Kevin. Mum says I'll learn someday.

So when Darren says his uncle's got pictures of dead people, I say what kind.

Darren sits up close to me. He smells dirty, but I don't tell him.

'You know,' he says. 'Shit you've seen on the telly.'

He pushes holes through my cigarette smoke then he tries to kiss me. I pull back. His teeth are yellow and there's a cold sore between his nose and his mouth. He sucks his tongue back in.

'I told him about you,' Darren says. 'I said you liked books and stuff. He said to bring you over sometime.'

So I go over.

Darren's uncle looks like Darren would look if he was in a book written by someone great. He lives in the garage because his wife hung herself after her baby died. Darren said I wasn't to mention anything about that. He said his uncle goes a bit crazy now and again and Darren's mum has to hide the knives and the bleach.

Darren's uncle smiles when he sees me. He puts his hand out for me to shake. I like his hand. It's very clean. He says, would you like a drink?

Darren goes over to a small fridge near a sink.

'Non-Alco,' Darren's uncle warns him.

Darren shrugs. 'Sure Eddie.'

His uncle gets me an orange juice. I'm trying to remember Darren's surname, while his uncle shoves some magazines off a chair.

'Thank, Mr Sheridan,' I say and sit down.

He bows a little. 'Eddie,' he says.

Darren says, 'I told her you had pictures of dead people.'

Darren's uncle looks funny at me.

'You don't have to show me,' I say.

Darren moves back and forward. 'No, he'll show you, won't you show them, Eddie?'

Darren's uncle shrugs. 'Okay.'

He goes over to a large bookshelf full of books. My eyes go fuzzy if I stare too much, but I want to see the names of the books. I want to open them up.

'I read books,' I say out loud.

Darren's uncle looks round at me.

'She reads to me,' Darren says.

I want to shut him up. I want him to disappear.

'That's good, that's nice,' Darren's uncle says.

He brings a large book over to his desk near the window. Darren gets there first, but his uncle makes a space for me between him and Darren. His uncle smells clean and just before I look at the picture he is showing me, I look at the side of his face. There's no hair on his cheeks at all and, this close to him with the light from the window, I can see that he has more red in his hair than brown, and his eyelashes are long and nearly red. Orange, but a nice orange. I smile a bit and he catches me.

I really hope I look like Darren says I do, like a girl from a painting in one of his uncle's books.

'I want a cigarette,' Darren says.

'Go on outside then,' his uncle tells him.

Darren goes outside and lights a cigarette in front of the window.

I look down at the picture his uncle is showing me. It's black and white and it has houses in straight lines. Nothing but houses, but weird houses. Long and narrow and with barbed wire wrapped around towers. I know what this is.

'Want to see the next one?'

'Sure,' I say.

I've seen pictures like these before in my history books. Darren's uncle goes through them all. He's counting the photograph pages under his breath. People who don't look like people anymore, dead people, piles of skeletons with bits of skin dripping off, women who still have ankle socks on their legs, even though they are dead and men's briefcases all buckled up.

Darren comes back in. 'What do you think?' he says.

I don't say anything. I drink my orange and walk about the room. Darren's uncle follows me. He touches some flowers in a vase then picks up a book. Darren leans against a wall and looks bored.

'You should get a telly in here, Eddie.'

'Don't want one.'

I'm standing in front of the books and Darren's uncle stands right beside me.

'You can read anything you like here,' Darren's uncle says. He looks at me. 'You can come back anytime.'

Afterwards Darren gets angry with me. He says maybe I want to fuck his uncle. I stop dead when Darren uses that word. It makes me go cold, right to my guts. Darren pushes me up against a wall and I want to scream, but his hand is over my mouth. Freda says she usually just ends up thinking about something else. Something like the dress she wants in Penny's. I think hard of nothing because the pain makes me want to break. Then I think of killing Darren. I think about finding a rock and smashing his face in two and when it's over I try so hard to walk like there is nothing wrong and Darren walks on ahead, smoking his cigarette and when I get home, I get into the hottest shower I can and I stay there until I can't feel anything anymore.

# Marsh

I was all bog and bits of islands,
my bird-heavy mane of reed
a river of lyrical russet,
a Celtic hunter slowing his currach
to the heartbeat of a wayward doe.

I grew wooden bridges and jetties,
ramparts and towers, cupped huts
and dirt roads. Smoke rose nightly
from the duels of swords and harps.

I sank heavier with merchants and markets,
cobblestones, cannons, kept alehouses then.
Top hats and summer umbrellas tilted
to soldiers and carriages. Oil street-
lamps lit stocks and paupers.
Men and metal stitched me whole.

Now I sleep with buses and pipes,
pylons and beggars reflected thrice in glass.
Mobile phones and mini-skirts flirt my name
while coffee-shop buskers point tourists to pavement art.

What will I not endure?

# Men Knitting

*after Lorca*

The men are hard at it, knitting
hats scarves and gloves
for a blood wedding.

Prolonged engagement, sitting
in hired rooms; push and shove:
the men are hard at it, knitting

the same pattern; no quitting,
inexorably the cord rises above
for a blood wedding

to end all seasons; as hard-hitting
comrades line up like collared doves.
The men are hard at it, knitting

by firesides and bonfires spitting
hot confetti: making the most of
'A Blood Wedding'.

While up the road, they're fitting
fresh coils of razor wool, with love.
Blood wedding, the men are hard at it
knitting…

PETE MULLINEAUX

# A Piper Prepares

It's almost like shooting up: a captivating ritual
as the belt is looped around the forearm, buckle
notched; blowpipe joined to leather bag; a shard
of cloth, folded between elbow and rib for comfort –

trusted talisman, guardian against the unknown
and unnamed – keys, bars with no endings. Drones
are attached like pistol silencers, regulators poised –
and now, the popping strap – the 'piper's apron'

a leather patch, spread across the thigh; you'd think
for protection from the crazed jabs of the chanter,
its manic hypodermic dance. In fact, the placing there
will cause a glottal stop, suspension of sound, a near-

death, allowing trap-door drop, down the pit-shaft
of the octave to low D: belly-forge, base underworld
from where a primal hum vibrates, connects –
fixes on the spinal cord, sends a hit exploding

into the skull's chamber. The head reels, a gasp
for air as the bellows fill and suddenly there's life
in the lungs and wind in the reeds, escape – we're
up and away – tripping over the scales, flying

above the Walls of Limerick, the never ending
Siege of Ennis – hello and goodbye to Rocky Road,
Wheels of the World, Hills and spills of Donegal –
heading towards that high high doh...

# Maple Spring

*Montreal 2012*

Poets bark out words in squares of red,
strange bubbles that float heavenwards
over island city streets, above Victorian
hospitals, lake of beavers, the cross.

Classical music explodes into the day
like slowly drifting cherry blossoms,
gathered into the echo of one single note,
the red of the rose with sharp thorns.

On the Metro a ballerina puts on a crimson dress,
starts a slow elegant pirouette, her energy
building, twirling into a tornado of creation,
a red wind whispers and blows on daily marchers.

Paint splatters the pavement, vermillion hands
grace bewildered buttocks of passers-by.
The statue Jeanne Mance has a make-over,
De Maisonneuve, in a new land, wears a red scarf.

But no one is muffled, speech is a lively fire
behind masks with curly mustaches, under
paper maché heads, behind banners – exposed,
youthful faces rejecting failures of our age.

When a ruby and violet sky darkens to black,
neighbours emerge into the summer night
to greet each other on steps and street corners,
sounding a discordant lullaby on pots and pans

and in the morning youthful feet stomp together
once more, bold, and without fear, as the redwing
blackbird in free flight; the path to a 'real' new world
simple as putting one foot in front of another.

# I Crept Out

It was half past eleven on a weeknight you were sleeping
and I thought the day was far from over but I felt it wouldn't
have much purpose however much I stretched it if the extra hours
I wrung out didn't involve you so I kissed your eyelids
then crept out in soft shoes and I stole this white-legged horse
for you. It wasn't easy and ever since his restless tail's been
flicking at the wet recesses of my eyes so you keep asking
if I'm crying but I can't answer because I always have to creep off
to distract him from his incessant foot stamping, in case you hear it
and while you watched the evening news I crept out to feed him
the spoils from our small kitchen. I gave him grapes and seeds
and oat flakes from my palm and I sang our song to calm him
while he was eating and I've been busy muffling up his snortings
with fake coughs  I've had to take up smoking so you don't hear him
blowing and suspect that I stole a colt and and have him stabled
in the bathroom of this two-up two-down brain. Some days when
I'm lonely he reaches me by neighing and it stays in my eardrums
reverberating so forgive me but at times I can't make out a word
you're saying and every day I get these surges of exhilaration
thinking how this chunky white-legged creature is the perfect
demonstration of how much I think you're worth and I can't stop
myself from visiting him, I creep out quite often now and I'm not
even missing the bits of our shared life I give him.

# lung

this is my thumb and index finger
and there is your earlobe between them
not the one with the freckle, the other –
(your head is on my chest) (lets make love)
this couch surrounds us and inside my tired head
it seems to rise and fall like us and our slow, synced breath
is thick with the heat of 40 LUCKY STRIKES
that we feel we never really wanted but
came with conversation, as always.
we have smoked too many cigarettes
and are now sitting in a big dark lung
alone but for the midnight taxis
and james bond on the television's screen
playing cards and failing to resuscitate his lover.

# Lucy Block Waited

When the doorbell rang I was in the TV room. We rarely had visitors. My mother didn't even like us coming home from school. So, casual callers were infrequent and unwelcome. I was usually forced to crawl on my belly to the front door like a child commando and to decipher who was outside. I incorporated forward rolls and somersaults to keep it interesting. The upper part of the door was beveled glass. Because of the distortion it could be have been a Martian or Marilyn Monroe or Mrs. Molloy from down the street (the least favored option). I relayed back to my mother, as she loitered in the kitchen doorway with a Sweet Afton in her hand and an anxious look, my best estimate of the enemy. If I guessed wrong I would be in trouble so I usually said it's the tinkers.

They can go and shite! She had a way with words. I liked the tinkers myself. Clutching the ragged manes of their piebald ponies, they rode bareback through our concrete streets, the metal of the horse shoes echoing off the valley of high rise flats, a high fidelity warrior sound on a lost trail. They rode their horses with majestic indifference and disdain. That's how I wanted to negotiate my way through my teens. But it didn't work out.

My mother learned Morse code when she worked in England so she instructed me how to tap on the door with the code THIS IS SEAMUS. She waited until the full sentence was keyed out before letting you in. This was hard when the wind and rain were chaffing the exposed skin of my skinny legs. I found a book in the library on Morse code so I started embellishing. THIS IS SEAMUS YOUR ONLY BEGOTTEN SON or THIS IS THE MILKMAN or THIS IS NOT A LOVE SONG or DIS IS A GALL-WAY AKCENT. Very fucking funny she would say when she eventually let me in. After a while she would swing the door open as soon as I got to THIS so the fun went out of it. I can still use Morse code if the need arises.

When I went to secondary school she gave me house keys. They were tied around my neck attached to my holy scapulars. She could think of nowhere safer. It was tricky because as you put the key in the door she was likely to pull it open quickly, pulling you inwards, the scapulars cutting into your neck, as you stumbled over the threshold. When you removed the key from around your neck she never yanked it open.

She also decided to end our isolationist policy. Glasnost was in effect. If the Russians could do it so could she. She was an avid news junkie. Now she wanted the door answered immediately in case we would miss anything. It was a bit late. Because of years of unanswered bells almost no neighbors called any more.

My mother shouted from the kitchen – get that will ya? I just ignored her. Sometimes she forgot especially if it was just one ring and she was drinking. Anyway my favorite program was starting – an hour long nature documentary on tropical predators.

After a few seconds when the bell rang again she walked to the doorway and pointing at me and then the door said

Answer that fucking door or I'll put you through it.

Fair enough. That beveled glass could ruin your complexion. She was dangerous when she was drunk.

Stop wearing that outfit – it gets on my nerves – if you want to live in the Amazon basin why don't you just fuck off there with yourself.

I was only thirteen so I thought it was a bit harsh. She could cut you with words like a blade through a baby rabbit. That is, the whole way through.

I wished I did live in the Amazon basin. I was wearing a safari outfit I bought at the St. Vincent de Paul shop on Sea Road. I wore it while watching nature and wildlife specials. The bell rang again.

She looked at the door and back at me.

The bell was ringing without cease now.

When I opened it I knew.

Knew I shouldn't.

Knew it was trouble, double trouble. The Block twins scanned me, blue black eyes, deep sea and no way back from full fathom five eyes, lost eyes, do-something-man and we'll pluck out your fuckin' eyes eyes.

Block A inspected me while he held his finger on the buzzer.

I'm here I said. He still held it depressed.

I felt like closing the door. Actually I felt like smashing it shut and nailing it up. I felt like puking. They instilled complete motor neuron function dysfunction once you were in range of them. They were lean and lethal and as steely as flick knives. They were sleek with venom and bravery and fighting power. They fought in silence – balletic street fighting kings, sculpting blows and kicks into a fierce pugilistic embrace, laying foes down on wet macadam, kissing with elbows and knuckles and knees and steel toe caps.

Anyway I was petrified. I felt like piercing their hearts with steel tipped arrows. I felt like levering those high-beam-light eyes out of their sockets so I wouldn't have to see them anymore. I had a crossbow in my room, I carried it around when Robin Hood was on TV. It might as well have been buried under the sea.

Block A stuck his boot in the doorframe. At least it wasn't my face. I looked down at the high polished boots. Block B leaned nonchalantly against the wall of the house, blowing cigarette smoke into the cool black night. With languorous rhythm and ease and skill he flicked opened and closed a butterfly knife. The moon glinted off its blade in high lustrous tints.

Block A: Doctor Fucking-eejit-ston I presume.

He laughed. I looked down at my safari outfit. At least he was au fait with the old African history and exploration stuff.

Block A: What the fucking fuck is that?

He pulled the butterfly net out of my hand. It burned my skin as he jerked it free. I used it as a prop with the safari ensemble. It was the nearest equivalent to a naturalist's insect net I could find. I forgot I was carrying it when I answered the door.

He showed it to Block B. Block A mimicked elaborate kung

fu stances making exaggerated ahh-soo sounds. Block B looked on impassively, just kept flicking his knife in the pale moonlight. Dancing in the moonlight. On this long hot summer night. Thin Lizzie I presume.

Block A then broke the bamboo pole of the net over his knee. It sounded like breaking a baby's back. He threw the pieces away into the wet street. You'll be next he said to me. I believed him.

Block A: My sister wants you to call over tomorrow night.

It could have been worse. I suppose.

What! you sure you have the right guy?

Yeah – we don't believe it either but that's it, you're it.

I'm not sure I can actually.

Actually, fuck you actually – you're her date until she says different, actually.

I would try to remember not to say actually again.

I don't get it

What don't you get?

I don't know – I just don't get it. I barely know her.

Well, you will soon, call around tomorrow night at 7.00. If you don't, you'll get it.

I knew what that meant. The other it. The blue-black, blood bruised, deep tissue, kicked to bits it.

He pushed me back against the wall. It had a pebble dash effect with nodules of rough concrete icing. My head hit against it with enough force for blood to run down from my scalp. I could feel it seeping down the back of my neck past the collar of my ensemble.

He removed his boot from the doorway.

OK safari-head – tomorrow at the house. Don't wear that gear.

Even I knew this.

When they got to the gate they looked back. They blew me kisses.

My mother came to the door.

What do the Blockheads want?

I was agitated.

Their sister wants me to call around tomorrow night.

So what? No need to have a meltdown. She's just a girl.

I moved past her. The smell of drink shrouded me.

Don't wear that outfit though she called after me.

Jesus Chrisssssssssst – I know – I know.

I tried to calm myself.

OK just a girl – just a girl – just a girl.

She wasn't.

Lucy Block was a warrior with pearl grey eyes, haughtiness cubed. She was like a warning beacon in the ocean of concrete and decay in Old Mervue. She shone until you sailed too close. Then you knew a hundred miles was too close. Ship aground, all hands lost. Caustic, filigreed defiance, life force shone off her. A rocker, king of the girls, brawler, sullen, muted, raging. Just my type. Not.

In the school corridors I watched for her. Her shaved head bobbing among a sea of students. Up scope, U boat love, depth charges away, U track her. She ignores you. Me.

I thought it was a trap or else that she liked me. Fuck. I avoided contact with girls. I didn't know where boys are from but girls were from Cubist – a planet out of my constellation. Girls scoped out the skies of emotion and feeling on elliptical orbits that I couldn't track. I had more of a chance of joining the Foreign Legion at fourteen (my number one ambition) as I had of negotiating the mental and social culverts of a date with Lucy Block.

My teenage aunt told me I was pale and interesting. I avoided the sun. She practiced dancing with me before she went out on Friday nights to trawl for an eligible skinhead at the local dancing emporium called The Kuru. So I could dance if I was stuck to impress I supposed. I had practiced the pogo for hours in front of the mirror. I could dance it all night if I had to. I felt like a Massai warrior as I practiced in my bedroom. I had great calf muscles after a few months. My mother would hammer on the ceiling.

Quit that fucking racket!

She gave up in the end. That fucker is nuts she said to her sister, my dancing partner aunt. My aunt blew smoke at the ceiling.

Nah – he's fine.

I missed half the life cycle of the python cleaning the blood from the collar of the safari jacket. Outside the dark night shimmered with Blades on street corners. My broken net lay on the wet concrete, hidden in the dark, forgotten. Butterfly knifes sang love songs. Lucy Block waited.

# Tea

The young man
teaches me
the art of tea.
First – hydrate
the leaves,
then pour into
the smelling cup.
It is sweet, no?
When you fill
the drinking cup
smell the empty one
– flowers.

            ,


When we met
on the street
after many years
you invited me
to your flat.
You brewed
Jasmine tea.

We crossed
the ha-penny bridge
together
that cold dry night
talking as if
we would both
be alive
for a long time.

            ,

What I remember
are the delicate,
almost translucent,
blossoms in the cup
you gave me –
like a window into
the spirit world
where you have
disappeared –

*Love
that ending.*

*Brilliant!*

# Graduation in Templemore

Uniform hats flung

        into clouds  of violently feckless

       ubiquitous blue

scatter brain cells abandoned

              into the East Munster wind

like confetti
      at the wedding

of the wolf

to the ewe.

# Memoirs of Woman's Aid

Most of all, I remember being lost yet unafraid
in fields of cereal wheat.
I remember my grandmother's throne in the kitchen,
both kettle and cooker within arms reach
her freshly cooked bread and slipper-clad feet.
My grandfather's shotgun, the smoke from his pipe
I remember running terrified to bed past the life-size statues
of Jesus and Mary twice my size
being followed to sleep by cold pious eyes
I remember little or nothing of Erin Pizzey
though I remember Anne Ashby quite well.

I remember my sister taking claim over my pram
sore legs screaming in the burning sun
Kildare by tractor, Cardiff beneath stage lights.
Walking amongst giants at the Welsh National Opera,
my Auntie Sheila's egg-in-a-cup.
I remember screaming at the clown
with his bucket full of everything you'd ever need
and nothing that you would, at Billy Smart's Christmas Circus.
I remember being six-years-old for the very first time
and what a great day that was,
picking my nose was something new
and there were tiger clubs at Dublin Zoo
but I remember little or nothing of the Chiswick High Road

I remember the white Christmas in Adelaide Road.
My police bike with its blue siren lights that flashed for one day
and I remember the children divorce courts refused
invincible, brazen and highly amused by our accents.
I remember my father-upon-Thames

dashing, drunken and charming to boot
flashing a smile as he waved us good bye
on the red London Bus for the very last time.

I remember it all, in super 8 vision,
my very first book and my father's last look.
I remember little or nothing of the rats that shared a cradle
with my baby sister, suckling on her bottle as she slept
in the derelict Palm Court Hotel where we sheltered
with the battered wives of Erin Pizzey's Woman's Aid.

# Francis Bacon and Samuel Menashe by Strange Coincidence

have bathtubs in the kitchen.
Bacon is dead.
I visit his studio Exhibition
in Dublin. It's Hallow'een.

Menashe, alive
up interminable flights
of stairs
in the corner
of my daughter's
sitting room
on DVD. See him recite

his poems seated on a red canvas chair.
I have one of my own
in orange
the bath beside him

he's too old for
he cannot step in.

Bacon from 'the order of chaos'
Menashe with 'no free will'
in thrall
hone incisions
cut to the bone.

# SUSAN LINDSAY

## Austerity

Red shawls
on the Masai hunter,
his apprentice.

Staffs and loin cloths,
bare feet shod
in open leather soles.

They walk for weeks
search for the antelope
prey to lions

whose first bites
leave blood tracks these
last Grassland Masters

seek out and follow
for days. Remaining
in sight.

'They think
we know nothing,'
the men whisper, laugh

at their own trackers –
a BBC film crew
*health and safety* fears.

Faced down by Masai intent
fifteen lions mauling
an antelope carcass

slink back
triggered to spring,
a circle of eyes watch,

as the hunters carve
off a leg, sling it
over shoulders

walk on.

# The Café

The best time here is this
heavenly lull between
elevenses and lunch hour
when I have all to myself
for company the waitress
who cannot stop finessing,
finessing. She repositions
a menu card; she pushes in
a chair; she reassembles
the cruets back into sets
that click smartly together;
she wakes up the flowers
of the day and makes them
stand taller in their vases.
(Only once has she spoken
half-personally to me, though
I didn't catch what she said.
It was the time a hail shower
cascaded out of a violet sky
darkening rapidly over the gables
of Shantalla, blew fiercely
across the car-parks, and whacked in
the doors, scattering the menu cards).

Though I always ask for one
coffee – regular, black – she
never presumes to guess.
And so each day is a new day.
Which is as it should be.
There is an understanding
that there is no understanding.
This way it remains a mystery

where one has to go when
one rises up, brow furrowed,
urgently checking the time
as one heads for the cash-desk.
There is some joy – more than
she can know – in dropping
the generous tip, nodding
and smiling and turning
clean away before the coin
stops spinning in the wine-glass.

# Brothers and Sisters

The fellows who travelled the farthest,
trudging in from the poorest townlands,
were the bravest and most obdurate of all.
They would not read, except sullenly, word
by hard-earned word; they would not spell,
except nerve-rackingly, letter by half-guessed
letter; they would not learn off verses, let alone
recite them in the sing-song way; they would not
nicely pronounce any word in which
their fathers' accents were disowned.
They brought upon themselves spectacular wrath.

They were struck, whole-handedly, across the face,
first on one side, then the other; they were cuffed,
suddenly and sharply, on the back of the head;
they had the sally rod made to slash and burn
across the fingers of both hands, which they barely
nursed
on their way back to their desks, their eyes barely
watering.
In the schoolyard they ran by themselves, ghosting
in and out of the trees that were out of bounds.

When the school day ended, they were the first
to the door. When their time was done, they were the
first
to leave the parish, making for London, Manchester,
or the US
where they always already had brothers and sisters.

# Rest

I drifted off for no longer, I am sure,
than half an hour or so, but I wake
to find the fire out, the room dark,
a shiver at my back, the light still on

in the dining room but no one there,
a hum of voices coming from somewhere
in the house – no, coming from a place
further off than the house can contain.

They're giving me time to heal,
but I can hardly wait for all life
to return, for the power to rise,
totter, toddle, shuffle, waltz, race

to where the warm and wicked laughter is.

*love it.*

# Threads

Like a hunchback on the floor,
Its shadow thinned by candlelight,
Faded jeans and jumpers fly,
Adding to its sloping height.

Each item wears its time of year,
From airy summer to winter-weight.
A flailing shirt falls to the floor,
Arms at the angle of ten-to-eight.

Stripes of blue and white emerge,
Print peeling from the chest,
A freckled face fills its hole,
Lips and hair once caressed.

Worn, but worn for something more
Than warmth, allegiance or style;
Memories and emotions woven in,
For now, it belongs to no pile.

I see character in all things worn:
The wire hanger bent out of shape,
The candle's wick drowning in wax,
The cotton neck's oval gape.

Those stripes still hang to the edge of a chair
As the hunchback is cleared away,
But every fabric sheds its skin,
And loosened threads will always stay.

*2012*
*Over the Edge*
*New Writers*
*of the Year*

## At Letterfrack

I still see him out there
in the fields at Letterfrack,
A beautiful, half-starved boy
skin drawn across his cheek.
Everybody knows him but
nobody lays claim to him,
As he goes about his work
pulling weeds from the earth.
His breath whispers in the
stones of the mountain side.
His hollow gaze follows me
across the fields as he works.
And even the trees are appalled
that I walk in such a place.

# Ending It

The worst part, if you want the sharp end of the truth of it, is that he has been on the verge of breaking up with her. He has mentally composed the text message, has even once typed it out in a tortuous crawl across the keypad. "I'm really sorry," it read, "but I've got a lot of shit going on at the moment. Don't think I can give you the attention you deserve. I think we should call it a day."

He knows it to be a weak variation on the it's not you; it's me theme.

It is, in any case, a supreme piece of half-truth. The shit he has going on is calculating a means of escape from the three-month affair with her.

And then the phone call. She speaks his name with a question mark. At once a thrill of foreboding shivers through him. They need to talk. His heart sinks, later perking at the prospect that she might be about to perform the dirty work herself. He hears the first pricking of tears in her voice as she rings off.

He comes to her place. At the door there is a perfunctory kiss. Her complexion, never sallow, has taken on an Addams Family hue. Without preamble, there in the hall, she announces in a cracking whisper, "I'm pregnant."

He is taken by a curious sensation as though his guts are spiralling through his body at breakneck pace. A kind of monochrome fizz, like television static, seizes his mind. Somewhere behind the haze a word is forming in bold upper case characters, primed for screaming, and the word has a brute eloquence, and is 'FUCK'. The word which emerges when the capacity for speech eventually returns is not this, but simply, "Okay."

He moves to hug her and the embrace is halting and wooden, as though performed by poor actors. It is a daytime soap opera hug. They move into the apartment's living room and she takes a corner of the couch, drawing her knees into her chest. She weeps briefly and he places a nervous weak hand on her leg.

"What do you want to do?"

"I'm going to England."

Relief. Some hormone or other goes to work, flushing cool relief through him. Guilt comes then, for the speed and force of his relief. It is trumped by the former emotion. A spectre had loomed, of a being he was responsible for, an elastic responsibility stretching backwards to the ghost child's creation and forwards to its life. The spectre was banished with the naming of a place, England. She would book a Ryanair flight from Dublin, have the business taken care of. He would buy her a large bouquet, place himself at her disposal for a decent interval. (Days? Weeks?) Then he would end it.

"Will you come with me?"

He hears the little girl fear in her voice, sees it in her pallor. He feels it in the quiver of limbs as he holds her. To his surprise, hugging becomes fondling and soon they are in her bedroom and clothes are cast floorwards. It is better than the awkward tangles they have formed before, more fluid and intense. After, he is sleepy and dozes. When he awakes she is back in the dark living room, glowing television blue. He says he will call her tomorrow and she says okay and glances at him before turning back to the TV.

By the time he phones the arrangements are made. Birmingham is the place.

He googles, curious despite himself. Three words become stuck in his brain, rattle around it like pebbles in a can. Manual vacuum aspiration. He does not like any of the words individually. Together they are a small but malevolent gang. There is an acronym, MVA, and this is better, but still sounds somehow militaristic. He knows he must never mention any of this to her.

On the way to the airport and on the flight and in the taxi to the place in Birmingham they hardly speak.

The driver must be well used to bringing Irish fares the few miles from the airport to this place, although, of course, there is no conversation. In fact, rather than speaking their destination, he has written the clinic's name and address on a scrap of paper torn from the airline magazine. The taxi man receives it without comment.

In the whizzing grey of the city's outskirts he asks how she is feeling and she nods and smiles thinly, without words. There is a ferocious paucity of speech on this ordinary West Midlands day. He himself feels a kind of exam morning tension, a tremulous wanting to have the thing over with.

He pays the taxi driver and the man, without looking, mutters something in a language he does not recognise.

He is obscurely discommoded by the clinic's banality. What had he expected, he chides himself, something Dickensian, forbiddingly institutional, decked in cobwebs and gargoyles?

At the front desk a receptionist performs a carefully regulated smile, not too broad but not too brief either. She is really rather attractive, this receptionist, and he feels a small stab of guilt and then disappointment that the guilt does not run deeper, to shame, even. But it does not. She is a pretty girl and he enjoys looking at her. The rutting urge has brought him, them, here and even now shows no sign of abating.

There is a form to be completed. The receptionist hands it, along with a biro, to Sara. Does he have to sign anything? As the father, if that's the correct word? No, of course not. Or does he? Where are the boundaries? Could he, if he so chose, call a halt to proceedings now? Would he raise the child alone? Would he, if it were an anatomical possibility, carry the child around for 36 weeks, face months of violent nausea and back pain and who-knows-what prior to the screaming sear of childbirth? No.

No, there is nothing for him to sign. And he resents this. The comparison is trite – his mind is flipping wildly today – but he recalls a recent party which he had no desire to attend but to which he was not invited. There was a hurt in the exclusion. He feels the same hurt now, feels it pulsing unspoken under his skin like his attraction to the receptionist.

Sara writes a false address on the form and he understands, feels a sudden wash of tenderness and wants to hold her. But he does not. He wishes they could slough off religion fully, like sodden clothes come in from the rain, but they cannot. They are damp with it still.

They are shown where to wait. The room is deathly. There is a scattering of lone women and a single man. Nobody looks up as they enter.

He inquires again how she is feeling and she snaps, if a whisper can be a snap, not to ask her that. She is right; the question is laughably flimsy, as useful as a paper raincoat. She will receive a local anaesthetic and so will be awake while the manual vacuum aspiration is performed. They have not discussed this. He has learnt it from the clinic's website.

The three gnarly words set up their rasp round his brain again. The waiting room walls are a cheerful shade of yellow. To occupy his mind he speculates on what this might be termed. Cornfield, perhaps, or Summer Glow. There are also three appalling paintings on the Cornfield / Summer Glow walls, of the sort sold in IKEA. They respectively depict a palm tree, a beach and some mountains. There are no human faces. He is pleased to find his sensibilities offended by the pictures, as this is a more manageable mental state. Indignation at poor taste he can handle. This pit-of-the-stomach stuff he cannot.

Then his phone rings. The tone is Enter Sandman by Metallica. His mother is calling. It is five or six fumbling seconds before he can silence the ring. A red wave of mortification sweeps his face. Sara shakes her head with slow anger. He mouths, "Sorry" to the waiting room but nobody is looking at him.

It shakes him, the fact of his mother's calling here, now. She does not know, of course. It nudges him closer to some kind of edge. Twenty-five, and still childhood forces he has fled – church, family – exert a pull upon him.

They call Sara's name. She half-turns to him, halts, rises from the tubular steel chair. Again he feels an urge to embrace her. Again he does nothing. Then she is gone.

He goes to the toilet. He vomits slightly. After, he feels better, not so much for the purging as for the physical penance it represents. Penance. A sickly floral air freshener scents the cubicle. It may as well be the snuff-scented must of a 1950s confessional. He is not so much ashamed as ashamed of being ashamed. He went on a march once, in college. Pro-choice.

He leaves the clinic for air and the noise of outside. The rush and hiss of traffic through puddles is a sweet music of distraction. He strolls along the footpath, doubles back, strolls again. He counts cars of particular colours. He buys a pack of Marlboro Red and smokes his first, second, third and fourth cigarettes in eight months. The light fades and thickens to gloaming. He returns.

Inside, the double doors leading to the private place are swinging and he catches a fragment of talk. "Lot of criers today, eh?"

Soon Sara is released from this private place. A nurse's hand is attached to her shoulder with professional compassion. The nurse leaves. He does not ask how Sara is feeling. She is wraith pale and trying hard to disguise a slight hunch in her posture.

There is a kind of perfunctory debriefing with another nurse. He – pointedly, he feels – is given condoms and leaflets concerning safe sex. She is given the contact details of counsellors – Irish, he notes – she may wish to call.

One of the safe sex leaflets features a pink anthropomorphic condom with thyroidal eyes, grinning mouth and stubby arms. He feels an absurd urge to punch the cartoon prophylactic – actually form a fist and strike the two-dimensional image right there in the clinic – prior to stamping on it from a considerable height. Of course, he does nothing, only nods with sombre concentration whilst the nurse speaks.

Outside, the evening has dimmed to inky darkness. They have some time before the flight home. There is an Indian restaurant nearby. He feels the sharp bite of scruples but is ferociously hungry. Physicality trumps the higher faculties once again. He nudges the words out, each shuffling tentatively behind its predecessor.

"Would you, eh, mind if I, or, eh, we, I mean, if you want, I don't know…"

He resorts to pointing to the neon Jaipur Palace sign. She nods with the effortful slowness of one underwater.

The restaurant is dead. He eats with zest and the food sings in him. She orders a naan bread and eats none of it. The air is lead between them. He feels her look at him once and thinks he sees contempt for his indecent appetite. But it is hard to fathom behind the matt painkiller finish of her eyes. Hard to fathom, all of this. All but one thing; there will be no need for him to end it now.

# Biographical Notes

ADAM WHITE read at Over the Edge in May 2012. He is from Youghal in east Cork. After many years working as a carpenter/joiner in Ireland and France, he developed an interest in teaching, and now lives in Normandy. His first collection of poetry, *Accurate Measurements*, was shortlisted for the Forward prize for best first collection in 2013.

AIDEEN HENRY read for Over the Edge in March 2007. Her debut collection of poetry, *Hands Moving at the Speed of Falling Snow*, was published by Salmon Poetry in 2010. She was shortlisted for the Emerging Poetry Section of the Hennessy XO Literary Awards. Her second poetry collection will be published in 2014. Her poems have been widely published in a number of literary journals including *West47*, *Crannóg*, *Stony Thursday Book*, *Revival*, *The SHOp*, *Ropes*, *Southword*, the *Cúirt Annual* and *The Sunday Tribune*.

AILEEN ARMSTRONG read for Over the Edge in September, 2011. Her work has appeared in numerous journals and anthologies, including *Galway Stories*, *The Stinging Fly*, and the *Long Story, Short*. She was the recipient of an Arts Council bursary award in 2010. *End of Days*, her first collection of short fiction, was published by Doire Press in 2013.

ALAN MCMONAGLE read for OTE in March, 2007. He has received awards for his work from the Professional Artists' Retreat in Yaddo (New York), the Fundación Valparaiso (Spain), the Banff Centre for Creativity (Canada) and the Arts Council of Ireland. *Liar Liar*, his first collection of stories, appeared in 2008 (Wordsonthestreet). The title story from his second collection, *Psychotic Episodes* (Arlen House, 2013), was nominated for a 2011 Pushcart Prize.

BRENDAN MURPHY read at OTE in October 2006. In the same year, he won the Cúirt Grand Slam and in 2007 he won the All Ireland Slam competition. His fiction has appeared in various anthologies both in Ireland and UK. His poetry collection *It's History* was published by Doire Press in 2010.

CAOILINN HUGHES read for the inaugural OTE event in January, 2003. Her first poetry collection, *Gathering Evidence,* will be published by Carcanet Press in February 2014, and concurrently by Victoria University Press in New Zealand, where she is completing a Ph.D. Poems from the collection won the 2012 Patrick Kavanagh Award, the 2013 Cúirt New Writing Prize and the Trócaire/ Poetry Ireland Competition.

CELESTE AUGÉ read for OTE in February 2005. She is the author of *The Essential Guide to Flight* (Salmon Poetry, 2009) and the collection of short stories *Fireproof and Other Stories* (Doire Press, 2012). Her poetry has been shortlisted for a Hennessy Award, and she received an Arts Council of Ireland Literature Bursary for her poetry collection *Skip Diving*. In 2011, she won the Cúirt New Writing Prize for fiction. She lives in Connemara in the West of Ireland.

DAVE LORDAN read for Over The Edge in April 2006. He is the first writer to win Ireland's three national prizes for young poets: the Patrick Kavanagh Award in 2005, the Rupert and Eithne Strong Award in 2008 and the Ireland Chair of Poetry Bursary Award in 2011 for his collections *The Boy in The Ring* and *Invitation to a Sacrifice*, both published by Salmon. His third collection of poetry, *Playing the Bones*, is published by Salmon in 2014.

DEIRDRE KEARNEY read for OTE in May, 2008. She is from Omagh and has lived in Galway since 1983. Her work has been published in various magazines, newspapers and anthologies. Her first collection of poems, *Spiddal Pier*, was published in 2010 by Lapwing Press, Belfast.

DONNA L. POTTS read for OTE in November, 2011. She is a professor at Washington State University who writes books about poetry, such as, *Howard Nemerov and Objective Idealism: The Influence of Owen Barfield* and *Contemporary Irish Poetry and the Pastoral Tradition*. She is grateful to people like Kevin Higgins and Susan Millar DuMars for encouraging her to write and publish her own poetry. Her debut poetry collection, *Waking Dreams*, was published by Salmon in 2012.

EAMONN HARRIGAN read for OTE in October 2008. He was shortlisted for the OTE New Writer of The Year in 2008. He holds a Masters in Screenwriting and was awarded a scholarship to UCLA Film School in 2009. Eamonn's debut fiction publication, *Where the Dead Go*, was published by Solstice Publishing in 2011.

EDWARD BOYNE read at Over the Edge in September 2005. He was shortlisted for the Hennessy award and the Francis McManus award. His first collection of poem, *The Day of the Three Swans*, was published in 2010 by Doire Press.

ELAINE FEENEY read at Over The Edge's fourth anniversary in January, 2007. She was born in Galway. Her two earlier collections of poetry were *Indiscipline* (Maverick Press) and *Where's Katie?* (Salmon Poetry). More recently Feeney launched a CD of her performance work with poet Sarah Clancy. Feeney has performed as a guest at many literary festivals internationally and her newest collection, *The Radio was Gospel*, was published in November 2013 by Salmon.

GARY KING read for Over The Edge in February 2003. He has had his poetry published in many magazines both in Ireland and the UK. In 2008, Gary was the winner of the second North Beach Poetry Nights Grand Slam. In 2007, he was joint runner up in the Cúirt International Festival Grand Slam. In 2013 he was shortlisted for the Cúirt New Writer Award in fiction. His debut poetry collection, *Pluto's Noon Sky*, was published in 2009 by Doire Press.

GER BURKE read for OTE in October 2004. She is a novelist and short-story writer. She has had many literary successes both in print and radio including being short-listed for the Francis McManus Short Story Award and long-listed for The Fish Short Histories Prize and the 2012 Fish Flash Fiction Competition. Her novel *My Father's Lands* was published in 2010 by Wordsonthestreet. *Braided Loves*, her new novel, was published in 2013. Ger is on the editorial board of *Crannóg*.

GERALDINE MITCHELL read for Over the Edge in February, 2009 and was chosen to read at the 2010 Over the Edge Showcase. Her debut collection *World Without Maps* was published by Arlen House in 2011 and reprinted in 2012. Geraldine won the 2008 Patrick Kavanagh Award. She was awarded an Arts Council Bursary in 2011. Her poems have been published in journals in Ireland, the UK and North America. She lives in Co. Mayo.

GERRY GALVIN read for OTE in December 2009. Originally from Limerick, he spent many years living in Oughterard, Co. Galway. He was a chef and former restaurateur, author of two cookbooks, *The Drimcong Food Affair* (McDonald Publishing, 1992) and *Everyday Gourmet* (The O'Brien Press, 1997). *No Recipe*, his debut collection of poetry, was published in 2010, and *Killer à la Carte*, a crime novel, was published in 2011, both by Doire Press. Gerry died on March 1, 2013.

GRACE WELLS read for OTE in February, 2004. Grace was born in London in 1968. Her first book, *Gyrfalcon* (2002), a novel for children, won the Eilis Dillon Best Newcomer Bisto Award, and was an International White Ravens' Choice. Other publications for children include *Ice-Dreams* (2008) and *One World, Our World* (2009). Her debut poetry collection, *When God Has Been Called Away to Greater Things* (Dedalus Press, 2010) won the 2011 Rupert and Eithne Strong Best First Collection Award and was short-listed for the London Fringe Festival New Poetry Award.

JARLATH FAHY read for OTE in March, 2006. He has been a member of Galway Writers' Workshop since 2000 and a member of the editorial board of *Crannóg* magazine since its inception. His poetry has appeared in *Criterion*, the Arts Society magazine and *Outlet*, the journal of the Philosophical Society NUIG. His first published collection, *The Man who was Haunted by Beautiful Smells*, was published by Wordsonthestreet in 2007. His next collection will be published in 2014.

JEAN FOLAN read for Over the Edge in November 2007. She is a Galwegian now living in west Sligo. Her first poetry collection *Between Time* (Lapwing) was published in 2013.

JENNY MCCUDDEN read for OTE in January 2008. She is the editor of *The Sligo Champion* and former TV3 Western Correspondent. She published a non-fiction book, *Impact* (Collins Press), in 2010. She was a featured reader in the Over the Edge Showcase at the Cúirt International Festival of Literature in 2009.

JIM MULLARKEY read at the inaugural OTE in January 2003. His work has been published in his short story collection *And* (2011) which was long-listed for the 2012 Edge Hill and Frank O'Connor awards. Short-listed and published in the 2012 Powers Irish Whiskey collection, Jim was previously short-listed for the R.T.E. Francis MacManus, and long-listed for the Raymond Carver and Fish short story competitions. He read in the Cúirt/Over the Edge Showcase in April 2006.

JOHN CORLESS read for OTE in March 2008. He writes poetry and drama. He plays three parts in 'The Pull,' a comedy play which he co-wrote with Liam Horan and which is touring nationwide. His short film, *Snap*, is due for release late 2013. His debut poetry collection, *Are You Ready?,* was published by Salmon in 2009 and he keeps threatening to publish another. He teaches creative writing and is Director of the Claremorris Fringe Festival of Drama.

JOHN WALSH read for OTE in April 2003. His first poetry collection, *Johnny Tell Them*, was published by Guildhall Press (Derry 2006). In 2007 he received a Galway County Council Publication Award for his second collection *Love's Enterprise Zone* (Doire Press). In 2010 Salmon Poetry published his latest collection *Chopping Wood with T.S. Eliot*. John received a second Galway County Council Publication Award for his debut short story collection *Border Lines* (Doire Press, 2012).

KATE O'SHEA read for OTE in October 2003. Short-listed for the Patrick Kavanagh Poetry Award 2012, this year her entry was chosen for special commendation. Riposte Books, Dublin, will publish her first collection in 2014. Recent poems feature in *CANCAN* (Scotland), *Lucid Rhythms* (U.S.A), *Angle Poetry Journal* (Australia), *www.thegalwayreview.com*, *Turbulence Magazine* (U.K.), *Poethead – Index of Women Poets*, and *Boyne Berries*. *Crackpoet*, published by Wurm Press, 2013, is available on Amazon.

KEVIN O'SHEA read for OTE in August 2009. He was shortlisted for Over The Edge New Writer of the Year in both 2009 and 2010. He has been published in *Irish Left Review*, *Ropes*, *Pen Tales*, *Northern Liberties Review*, and *The Living Link*. In 2012 he was the winner of the Cúirt New Writing Prize, Poetry Award and his debut collection *The Art of Non-Fishing* was published by Doire Press. He is co-editor of the poetry newspaper *Skylight 47*.

LORNA SHAUGHNESSY read for OTE in December 2003. She was born in Belfast and lives in Co. Galway. She has published two poetry collections with Salmon Poetry, *Torching the Brown River* (2008) and *Witness Trees* (2011). She lectures in Hispanic Studies in NUI, Galway. She has contributed to anthologies of Galician poetry and has published three collections of Mexican and Galician poetry in translation.

MARTIN DYAR read at Over the Edge in October 2010. He was the winner of the Patrick Kavanagh Poetry Award in 2009, and the Strokestown International Poetry Award in 2001. In 2010 he was selected for the Poetry Ireland Introductions Series. He has been the recipient of two Arts Council Literature Bursary Awards. He is currently a member of the International Writing Program at the University of Iowa. Martin's debut collection, *Maiden Names*, was published by Arlen House in 2012.

Mary Madec read for Over the Edge in November, 2005. She has received awards and accolades for her work in the Raftery Competition 2007, the WINDOWS Showcase and Anthology 2007 and the Maria Edgeworth Competition 2008. In April 2008 she was also the recipient of the Hennessy XO Award for

Emerging Poetry. Mary's debut collection, In Other Words, was published by Salmon in 2010. Her next poetry collection, *Demeter Does Not Remember*, is forthcoming from Salmon.

MICEÁL KEARNEY read at Over The Edge in September 2006. He lives in South Galway. He has been published in Ireland, England and America, and read as part of Poetry Ireland's Introduction Series in 2009. Doire Press published his debut collection, *Inheritance*, in 2008. In 2013 he wrote and directed his first play, *Never Ending Wild Stories*, as part of the Claremorris Fringe Festival.

MICHELLE O'SULLIVAN read for OTE in February 2008. She lives in Mayo. She was the winner of the Strong/Shine Award for her collection *The Blue End of Stars*, published in 2012 by Gallery Press.

NICKI GRIFFIN read for OTE in September 2010. She won the OTE New Poet of the Year competition in 2010. In 2012 she was awarded a Literature Bursary by the Arts Council. Her debut poetry collection is *Unbelonging*, published by Salmon in 2013. A non-fiction work, *The Skipper & Her Mate*, was also published in 2013 by New Island Books. Nicki is co-editor of the poetry newspaper *Skylight 47*.

NOEL DUFFY read for OTE in April, 2004. He was shortlisted for both the Over the Edge New Writer of the Year Award and the Patrick Kavanagh Poetry Prize in 2010. His debut collection, *In the Library of Lost Objects*, was published by Ward Wood, London, in 2011 and was shortlisted for the Strong Award for best first collection by an Irish poet. His second collection, *On Light & Carbon* (Ward Wood), was published in late 2013.

ÓRFHLAITH FOYLE read for Over The Edge in May 2003. Her first novel *Belios* was published by The Lilliput Press (2005), and her first full poetry collection *Red Riding Hood's Dilemma* published by Arlen House (2010) was short listed for the Rupert and Eithne Strong Award in 2011. Her debut short story collection, *Somewhere in Minnesota*, was published by Arlen House in 2011; the title story was first published in Faber and Faber's *New Irish Short Stories* (2011), edited by Joseph O'Connor.

PAUL CASEY read for OTE in March 2010. His chapbook *It's Not all Bad* (Heaventree Press) was published in 2009. In 2010 his poetry-film *The Lammas Hireling* (after Ian Duhig), premiered in Berlin. His collection *home more or less* was published by Salmon Poetry in 2012. He is the founder / organiser of the Ó Bhéal reading series in his home city, Cork.

PETE MULLINEAUX read at OTE in December 2003. His work has been widely anthologised, including in *Poetry & Song* (Macmillan), *Poetry Ireland Review* 100 (ed. Paul Muldoon), *about.com/poetry* and *Poetry Daily* (USA), *Van Gogh's Ear* (Paris). Pete has also had a number of stage plays produced, including *Trust Games* (Irish National Association of Youth Theatres) and three dramas for RTÉ radio, most recently *Butterfly Wings*, 2011. His first collection, *A Father's Day*, was published by Salmon in 2008; it was followed by *Sessions* in 2011 (also from Salmon).

SANDRA BUNTING read for Over the Edge in March, 2004. She recently co-wrote *The Claddagh: Stories from the Water's Edge*, published by The History Press, Dublin. *Identified in Trees*, her poetry collection, appeared in 2006 by Marram Press. Awarded a 2012 Glenna Luschei award for poetry, she was also runner-up for the 2006 Welsh Cinnamon Press First Novel Competition and a finalist for the 2009 Irish Digital Media Awards for her Blog: Writing a Novel Online. Sandra sits on the editorial board of *Crannóg* magazine.

SARAH CLANCY read at OTE in August 2010. She has written two collection of poetry; *Stacey and the Mechanical Bull* (Lapwing Press 2011 ) and her current collection *Thanks for Nothing, Hippies* (Salmon Poetry 2012). Her poems have been published in Ireland and abroad. She has won many Irish poetry competitions for both performance and page poetry, and been shortlisted for both the Listowel Collection of Poetry Competition and the Patrick Kavanagh Award. Her third collection is forthcoming from Salmon.

SARAH GRIFF read at Over The Edge in January 2010. Her work has appeared in *The Irish Times*, *The Rumpus*, and *The Stinging Fly*, and she has read multiple times on RTÉ Radio's arts programme, *Arena*. She is co-editor of *Bare Hands International Poetry Journal*. Her first collection of poetry, *Follies*, was published by Lapwing in 2011, and her collection of essays, *Not Lost*, was released by New Island in Winter 2013.

SEAMUS SCANLON read for OTE in May, 2011. He is a librarian at City College's Centre for Worker Education in New York. Highlights: winning OTE and Fish One Page Story contests, publication of *As Close As You'll Ever Be* (Cairn Press, 2012), Centre for Fiction fellowship, a residency at MacDowell, book launch at Charlie Byrne's, publication in *Mondays are Murder* (Akashic Books), and the *Artistic Atlas of Galway*.

SHEILA PHELAN read for OTE in January, 2005. Born in Dublin in 1971, she received an MA in Writing at NUI, Galway in 2003. Awards include an Arts Council Bursary in 2002 and second place in the Patrick Kavanagh Competition 2005. An essay on Yeats and the Abbey Theatre was published in New Hibernia Review in Fall, 2006. Sheila Phelan currently lives in New York with her husband and two children. Her collection *Washington DC* was published by Lapwing in 2007.

STEPHEN MURRAY read for Over the Edge in September 2005, as Cúirt Grand Slam Champion. He is the author of two collections of poetry with Salmon Poetry – *House of Bees* (2011) and *On Corkscrew Hill* (2013) – and his work has appeared in journals worldwide. He lives in the West of Ireland where he writes and works as the director of Inspireland, providing arts and literacy programmes for secondary schools showcased in the online magazine *Brave New Words*.

SUSAN LINDSAY read for OTE in March 2006. In 2011 her debut collection of poetry, *Whispering the Secrets*, was published by Doire Press and she read for the Poetry Ireland's Introductions Series. She has read at Over the Edge, the Belfast Book Festival, Cúirt Literary Festival, Clifden Arts Week and on RTÉ radio. She is currently one of three co-editors of the poetry newspaper *Skylight47*. Susan's second collection, *Fear Knot*, was published by Doire in October 2013.

TOM DUDDY read for OTE in March, 2006. He taught Philosophy in the School of Humanities at NUI Galway. His academic publications include *A History of Irish Thought* and *Dictionary of Irish Philosophers*. Tom contributed to Irish and British magazines, such as *Poetry Ireland Review, Magma, Smiths Knoll, The Dark Horse, The Rialto* and *The Frogmore Papers*. His chapbook, *The Small Hours*, was published in 2006, and his first full collection, *The Hiding Place* (Arlen House), in 2011. Tom Duddy died on June 15, 2012.

TREVOR CONWAY read for OTE in October, 2009. He writes mainly poetry, fiction and songs. His first collection of poetry, *Evidence of Freewheeling*, is forthcoming from Salmon Poetry, while another two collections are near completion. An album of his songs (some based on poems) was released in 2013, titled *Morning Zoo*. He's a contributing editor for *The Galway Review*, and his work has appeared in Ireland, England, Scotland, Austria, the US and Mexico.

## Over the Edge New Writers of the Year, 2012

FIONA SMITH is a translator and journalist. She reports on Irish news for the German Press Agency dpa and translates from Scandinavian languages. She has had poetry published in *Southword* and in *Hennessy New Irish Writing*. She won the poetry section of the 2012 Over the Edge New Writer of the Year competition with "At Letterfrack". She lives in Kinsale, County Cork.

SEÁN KENNY's fiction has appeared in *Crannóg, The Irish Times*, New Irish Writing in *The Irish Independent, The South Circular, Southword* and *Wordlegs*. He won the 2012 Over The Edge New Writer of the Year competition and is shortlisted for a 2013 Hennessy Literary Award. His story, "Ending It", was recorded and broadcast by RTÉ Radio One in June 2013 as the third-placed entry in the Francis MacManus Short Story Competition.

# Acknowledgments

All poems and stories in this anthology are copyright of their authors. Over the Edge and Salmon Poetry also wish to acknowledge and thank the following publishers and journals where some of the poems in this anthology were first published:

ADAM WHITE: "Learning to Cast" and "Her and that Wardrobe" from *Accurate Measurements* (Doire Press, 2013).

AIDEEN HENRY: "Mary Ferriter" from *Hands Moving at the Speed of Falling Snow* (Salmon Poetry, 2010).

AILEEN ARMSTRONG: "Today" from *End of Days* (Doire Press, 2013).

ALAN MCMONAGLE: "Bloomsday Bus Driver" from *Psychotic Episodes* (Arlen House, 2013).

BRENDAN MURPHY: "Slum Pottery" from *It's History* (Doire Press, 2010).

CAOILINN HUGHES: "Avalanche" has also appeared in *Landfall*, produced by Otago University Press (issue 244, November 2012).

CELESTE AUGE: "I Dream in Solid Pine" from *The Essential Guide to Flight* (Salmon Poetry, 2009). "Brigit (the Accidental Bishop)" has appeared in *Skylight 47* (Issue 1, 2013).

DAVE LORDAN: "Fearless" from *The Boy in the Ring* (Salmon, 2007).

DEIRDRE KEARNEY: "Peace Fire" from *Spiddal Pier* (Lapwing Press, 2010).

DONNA L. POTTS: "Tiananmen Square" from *Waking Dreams* (Salmon, 2012).

EAMONN HARRIGAN: "Night Watchman" from *Where the Dead Go* (Solstice Publishing Ltd., 2011).

EDWARD BOYNE: "Tribe" also appeared in *Watching My Hands at Work: A Festschrift for Adrian Frazier* (Salmon, 2013).

ELAINE FEENEY: "Urban Myths and the Galway Girl" from *Where's Katie?* (Salmon Poetry, 2010).

GARY KING: "Contact" from *Pluto's Noon Sky* (Doire Press, 2009).

GER BURKE: *My Father's Lands* was published by Wordsonthestreet, 2009.

GERALDINE MITCHELL: "Lull" from *World Without Maps* (Arlen House, 2011). The poem first appeared in the 2009 Oxfam Calendar.

GERRY GALVIN: "Give Me the Eyes of a Stranger," "Milestone" and "Trstenik, Croatia" are used with the kind permission of the Galvin family.

GRACE WELLS: "The Work" and "Pioneer" from *When God Has Been Called Away to Greater Things* (Dedalus, 2010).

JARLATH FAHY: "the day I fell in love with a housecoat in otooles supervalu tuam the haberdashery section" from *The Man who was Haunted by Beautiful Smells* (Wordsonthestreet, 2007).

JEAN FOLAN: 'Absence' from *Between Time* (Lapwing, 2013); first published in West 47 online, 2006.

JENNY MCCUDDEN: 'Pride' from *Three Times Daily* (NUIG anthology, Dublin Original Writing Ltd., 2010).

JIM MULLARKEY: "Heaven" from *And* (Doire Press, 2011).

JOHN CORLESS: "Are You Ready?" from *Are You Ready?* (Salmon, 2009).

JOHN WALSH: "A Beautiful Day" from *Border Lines* (Doire Press, 2012).

KATE O'SHEA: "Story of Lug" from *Crackpoet* (Wurm Press, 2013).

KEVIN O'SHEA: "New Trick for Jessie" was previously published in Skylight Poets' 2011 anthology *Mosaic* and is from *The Art of Non-Fishing* (Doire Press, 2012).

LORNA SHAUGHNESSY: "Carran" and "Vantage Point" from *Witness Trees* (Salmon, 2011).

MARTIN DYAR: "Death and the Post Office" and "Independence" from *Maiden Names* (Arlen House, 2012).

MARY MADEC: "In Other Words" from *In Other Words* (Salmon, 2010).

MICEÁL KEARNEY: "Larry and Barry" appeared in *Cyphers,* Winter 2009.

MICHELLE O'SULLIVAN: "An Unknown Blue" from *The Blue End of Stars* (Gallery Press, 2012).

NICKI GRIFFIN: "Shoreditch" appeared in *Crannóg* (Autumn 2012). It is from the collection *Unbelonging* (Salmon Poetry, 2013).

NOEL DUFFY: "The Horologist's Dream of Silence" from *In the Library of Lost Objects* (Ward Wood, 2011).

ÓRFHLAITH FOYLE: "Dead People" from *Somewhere in Minnesota* (Arlen House, 2011).

PAUL CASEY: "Marsh" appeared in the *Cork Literary Review* (2009). It is from the collection *home more or less* (Salmon Poetry, 2012).

PETE MULLINEAUX: "Men Knitting" from *A Father's Day* (Salmon Poetry 2008). "A Piper Prepares" from *Session* (Salmon 2011).

SANDRA BUNTING: "Maple Spring" appeared on the *One Hundred Thousand Poets for Change* website, 2011.

SARAH CLANCY: "I Crept Out" appeared in *The Moth* (2012). It is from the collection, *Thanks for Nothing, Hippies* (Salmon Poetry, 2012).

SARAH GRIFF: "Lung" from *Follies* (Lapwing, 2011).

SEAMUS SCANLON: "Lucy Block Waited" is a shorter version of "Butterfly Love Song" from *As Close As You'll Ever Be* (Cairn Press, 2012).

SHEILA PHELAN: "Tea" from *Washington, D.C.* (Lapwing, 2007).

STEPHEN MURRAY: "Memoirs of Women's Aid" from *House of Bees* (2011, Salmon Poetry). "A Graduation in Templemore" from *On Corkscrew Hill* (Salmon Poetry, 2013).

SUSAN LINDSAY: "Francis Bacon and Samuel Menashe by Strange Coincidence" from *Whispering the Secrets* (Doire Press, 2011). 'Austerity' from *Fear Knot* (Doire Press, 2013).

TOM DUDDY: "The Café", "Brothers and Sisters", "Rest" from *The Hiding Place* (Arlen House, 2011).

TREVOR CONWAY: "Threads" appeared in *Measured Words* (anthology, NUIG MA in Writing, 2010). It is from his forthcoming poetry debut, *Evidence of Freewheeling* (Salmon Poetry).